DAVID EVANS

REMEMBERING THE SOOS

Remembering The SOOS

david evans

PLAINS PRESS

A NOTE

The events of this book are true, but some of the names of the people have been changed.

"Remembering the Soos" appeared first in *South Dakota Review*; "Place of Your Dreams" appeared first in *Another Season*. The author is grateful to the editors of these journals for their permission to reprint those essays here.

Photo credits: cover photograph and photographs on pages 50 (Don Ward, David Evans, and Larry Johnson), 60, 66, 70, 74 and 77 courtesy David Evans; photos on pages x, 15 and 18 courtesy John Uber; photos on pages 23, 25, 29 and 87 courtesy Paul Fleckenstein; photo of David Evans on back cover courtesy Jan Evans; photo on pages 16-17 courtesy Sioux City Museum.

Cover design by David Pichaske.

Typesetting by Gail Perrizo and the Minneota (MN) *Mascot*.

Printed by M & D Printing, Henry, Illinois.

Published by Plains Press, Southwest State University, Marshall, Minnesota 56258.

Publication of this book is made possible by a grant from the Otto Bremer Foundation of the First American Bank and Trust, for which our many thanks.

ISBN 0-918461-05-X

For my mother, who said I should write a book
For my bothers Jerry and Bob, and my sister Judy
For my wife Jan
For my children Shelly and David and Kari
For my grandson Dustin
And in memory of my father and sister Bonnie

REMEMBERING THE SOOS

''The ball I threw while playing in the park
Has not yet reached the ground.''

—Dylan Thomas

Remembering The Soos

1

I was a boy running at night, inside a yellow river of headlights, running alongside the slow, bunched-up cars flowing out of the main parking lot of the baseball park after a game. I was running and breathing easily. My light-footed steps on the gravel shoulder blended with the kicked-up dust and reddish exhaust and the ticking gravel that sounded like grasshoppers popping around in dry weeds. I was in no hurry; I was saving up my energy. I was just going home like everybody else. In my right hand was a baseball. Now and then a car honked at the one in front of it, or at me.

The river of headlights divided, at 11th and Steuben, into two rivers: one kept flowing south toward the South Bottoms, a neighborhood near the packinghouses; the other—the one I took—turned right and headed toward the Wall Street bluff and the west and north parts of town. The noise of the traffic was cut almost in half. I had to quicken my pace because now there were fewer cars to run with, and they were moving faster.

I ran past the gravel company, past the soybean mill with its odor of baking soybeans, over the four sets of railroad tracks east of the mill, past two empty boxcars under the bluff—the light from headlights shooting through their open doors—then hurried up the steep, one-block hill that ended with a stop sign on Wall Street, my street.

The river of traffic flowed on, car by car, through the stop sign, dividing again, this time in three ways: straight ahead toward Court Street and the West Side, left for downtown, and right, up Wall Street. I turned right, ran about 10 more yards, and stopped beside a telephone pole. I was not winded, even *after the run up the hill. I had discovered a steady, untiring pace. But my heart was pounding anyway, through my hand held on my chest. I would wait a few minutes, settle down, before I started again. That was my habit.*

Now I was on top of the bluff. I stepped up on the curb and looked back across the valley. Except for a few lights on utility poles, and the lights of the stadium, which lit only the ball park itself and the sky over it, the valley was dark. There was no moon because of clouds—grey streaks—so I couldn't see the shiny railroad tracks running out to the end of the horizon and over it, south to Omaha.

But I knew where things were. The roundhouse with all its pigeons cooing or asleep inside the rafters of the flat, tarred roof. The pyramids of gravel and sand inside the high mesh fence of the gravel company. The small rat pond with those tensely-pinging powerlines above it. I tried to fix my sight on the exact places for all these things—even that lone boxcar just north of the roundhouse. It had to be there too, with its sides busted out like a bloated cow because it had stood too long in Missouri flood water.

I looked at the empty ball park a mile away. A smoky haze, like a low cloud, hung over the brown infield and green outfield. Soon the line of cars from the parking lot would be gone. Then a few minutes later the stadium lights would go out, and the whole valley would be black. I watched until the last car was leaving. I wondered what the driver was thinking. Did he know he was both the beginning and the end of a river?

I had two blocks to go—one block downhill, one block uphill—mostly in the dark because very few cars were going up Wall Street now. I stepped off the curb onto the pavement, and leaned toward home like a runner poised under a starting pistol. It wasn't exactly fear that I felt. It was the anticipation of the fear that would be running with me when I got to the bottom of the hill. It was like being on a roller coaster at the top of the ride, above the trees and about to start down. You know your guts will drop and your breath will be sucked out as you fall. It would be like that, without the wild screaming of the girls and the clattering of steel wheels on steel tracks.

With springy steps I crossed the street to the sidewalk and broke into a half-sprint just as a car turned down the hill behind me. *Running downhill was easy; all I had to do was lengthen my stride and relax. Yet if I relaxed too much my legs would jolt me as if I was running on stilts.* The car coasted the *first half-block, then as I levelled out on the brief strightaway its momentum carried it past me and the lights flashed by. A second car was gaining on me now, and as I shortened my stride into a full sprint, uphill now, suddenly fear was running with me. Fear was not a shape; it was the sound of footsteps, my footsteps, that I could speed up or slow down at will. The second car's headlights flashed past me just as I hit the incline at top speed. No headlights replaced the last ones so I was running in a gap of darkness. I knew by the sound of my steps on the brick sidewalk—the lightness, the intervals—exactly how fast I had run before and how fast I was going now, and I was surprised at my speed. I couldn't outrun the fear, but I could make it run faster than ever. My knees were pumping almost chest high, my gym shoes ticking over the smooth bricks. When I got to the alley I flew across it without glancing down its black throat, then reached the picket fence of my house, vaulted over it on one hand and leaped onto the cement porch.*

The fear was gone. No lights were on. Everybody was in bed. Breathing hard, I steadied myself on one knee close to the porch swing, and felt my heart again. It was still flying up the sidewalk on light legs.

Upstairs in my bedroom, I tossed my new baseball on my bed. I opened my dresser drawer and reached in under the rolled-up socks and folded tee-shirts and pulled out the other balls, filled my stretched-out shirt with them, and dropped them all on the bed. I arranged them in a row from oldest to newest, smudgy to clean white. Twelve balls. I could almost count my birthdays with them. I jumbled them together on the bedspread to see if I could spot the new one. I could. It was the shiniest. I picked it up and turned it over in my hands, feeling the hard seams and rubbing it down the way an umpire does. I smelled the white leather mixed with palm sweat.

I gathered all the balls in my shirt again and put them back in the drawer, and closed it. I undressed, switched off the light and got into bed. I watched the little pasted silver stars on my

3

*ceiling gradually appear. Now and then the headlights of a car
flattened out and slid over the ceiling and down the wall. A few
minutes later, facing the open window, I saw the faint glow in
the sky over the Cardwell roof across the street and over the
valley, go out. That was the ball park lights. I wondered, as I
often wondered: do the lights make a noise when they go out?*

2

Thirty years away, when I remember the Sioux City Soos'
ball park, it's the sounds that come back first. The spirited,
piercing, two-tone whistle of the left fielder, immediately
followed by "Come babe" — an exhortation to the pitcher. The
call of the pop vender making his way through the grandstand
and box seats: "Iiiiiice cold pop! . . . Iiiiiice cold pop!" — and
sometimes, the smart-aleck, anonymous echo: "Taaaaastes
like slop!" The theme song on the P.A. system before the
game, during warmups:

> Sioux City Sue,
> Sioux City Sue,
> There ain't no gal as true
> As my Sweet Sioux City Sue

And, from the roof over the grandstand, the lofty voice of the
captain of the ball shaggers, after a ball has popped up over
the stadium lights and is about to land with a chunky thud on a
shiny car top in the parking lot: "Overrrrr!" And then the
chunky thud.

The taste of water from the men's restroom comes back
too — the best water I've ever had. If you weren't careful when
you turned the loose knob, the sudden blast could knock the
little cone-shaped dispenser cup out of your hand and soak
your clothes. What worked best — and is still the way I prefer
to drink water — was to stick your head in the sink and use one
or both hands for a cup. The water was so cold it made my
teeth ache. I couldn't get enough of it; I drank until my
stomach hurt.

Several friends and I used to hang around that ball park in
our early teens, in the early 50s. The Soos were a class A farm
club in the old Western League that included teams from such

4

far-away places as Colorado Springs, Pueblo, Wichita, and Des Moines.

Just outside the right-field fence was a line of trees running along a creek. We could always sneak in. We usually waited until just before the game started; then, with a ball glove dangling on a wrist, we climbed a tree, dropped over the fence and scattered slick as rats into the moving crowd. Or if we were already in the park when the game started, as we often were, it didn't make sense to have to pay, so we didn't. As the season waned, the game cop gave up chasing us out when he saw us topping the fence. He would simply look the other way, knowing we had a dozen more entrances. Sometimes just to look respectable we'd buy tickets and walk through the front gate with honest faces. But that was rare.

There was a definite pecking order among the boys who came to the games. The youngest ones in their pre-teens usually stayed in the bleachers, watching the game and waiting, big-eyed, for foul balls. They couldn't keep any ball they happened to catch or retrieve, unless they could quickly turn it over to an adult they knew in the crowd. They were scramblers. Whenever a ball was driven or popped into the bleachers, they were after it like crazy sharks.

A second group, which my friends and I were part of, not only watched the game but played catch behind the bleachers, got to know some of the players by running errands for them—getting them cokes, chewing tobacco or cigarettes from the concession stand—and moved freely around the park, both outside and inside the fence. We couldn't keep the game balls we retrieved either, but we could take home a practice ball now and then, if it was water-soaked or too beat up to use for batting practice.

At the top of the pecking order were the shaggers, those hired to retrieve balls. Because they were the oldest, and usually the biggest and toughest, we made sure they could tolerate us. They didn't quite have the authority to kick us out if we acted up, but they could man-handle us if they needed to. We too wanted to be shaggers when we turned 16 and were eligible for work—and be paid for having all that prestige—and so we made their job easier by helping them chase balls. Up to a point, anyway.

The captain of the shaggers for a couple of seasons was a big, barrel-chested, awkward guy named Sam Hastings. Sam lived in my neighborhood on the Wall Street bluff and was in high school while I was still in Woodrow Wilson Junior High. He was dependable and commanded respect. His position during a game was on top of the long roof over the grandstand. From that height he had a panoramic view of the action and would shout down his instructions to the other shaggers. Though there were chairs on the roof, he never sat down. He kept shambling back and forth like a bear, always ready with each pitch to follow the ball wherever it might go.

Sam had several other shaggers under him: one or two in the bleachers; one in the front parking lot; one on the scoreboard; and often a "floater" who had to get the balls from the others and relay them up to the roof. The scoreboard shagger had the extra job of shoving the big slate numbers, usually zeros, into the slots after each half-inning. It was a privilege to be able to stand on the scoreboard catwalk with the shagger. With your head stuck through an empty square hole, you had an excellent view of the game, and might even start up a conversation with the right fielder, who always seemed bored because he was so far from the action.

But Hastings on the roof had the best view of the game, and he was in control. Any balls we got hold of had to go to him. Even though every shagger except the one in the parking lot could see the ball off the bat and respond to it on their own, Hastings made everything official with his shouting. When a ball went over the left-field fence, fair or foul, he shouted "Leffffft!" When a homerun ball was driven far enough over the left- or center-field fence to make the dump (Dick Stuart of Denver, who later starred for the Pittsburgh Pirates, had the habit of slugging the ball over the flag pole at the 402-foot mark in dead center), the word was "Dummmmmp!" When a ball barely cleared the right-field fence, the word was "Creeeeek!" (We pronounced it "crick" but when you shouted it the "ee" sound carried better.) The shaggers knew where the ball was going, could see it with their own eyes. That's what they were being paid for. And yet Hastings kept shouting the obvious.

I resented him for it. He was, I suppose, one of the first non-adults in my life, not including my older brother, who could make me do something I didn't necessarily want to do. I resented him also—and envied him—because he was being paid to watch the game. How could a person get paid for having such a good time? And yet he always looked too serious and busy to be enjoying the game.

Sometimes I would sit alone on a tree limb outside the fence, leering up at Hastings. He wasn't looking at me; he had work to do, and who was I to him but another punk waiting for a chance to steal a ball? I shouted at him, not loud, from my safe perch.

"You bastard you!"

If I ever caught his eye, nothing came of it. Hastings got to know which batters hit the most foul balls and homeruns. When they were at the plate he tensed up with each pitch. When the batter swung and missed, his tension released itself in body english.

A shagger could never throw a ball back onto the playing field unless the umpire or a player called for it. Between innings, when he had accumulated four of five balls, Hastings rolled them one by one down the screen stretched over the grandstand to the bat boy—a clean kid named Denny in a clean white uniform—who gave them to the plate umpire, who inspected them, rubbed them down and, if they were still useable, dropped them into the ball bag slung from his waist like a sower's pocket.

Catching or chasing after foul balls or homeruns was sheer joy. Getting your hands on a brand-new baseball was like suddenly finding a huge diamond. And it was a challenge, since all of us wanted to be the one who got to the ball first and then turned it over to a shagger. If you were fast enough and rough enough with your elbows and were able to retrieve several balls in one game, you might even be in line for a shagging job. Once, standing near the bleachers, I reached up to snag a towering foul ball, with everybody watching, and the ball grazed my glove and struck me in the left eye, knocking me out. When I came to, somebody was holding a chunk of ice on my eye.

But there was another, hairier challenge: to be the first one to the ball and, with nobody watching, to nonchalantly kick it into a clump of weeds or under a board and hope that it wouldn't be found. Then you would try to lure the others to some other spot where you were *sure* you saw the ball land. After the game you would go back and find the ball and take it home. It didn't work often, but I managed to squirrel away my share of balls over several seasons. The excitement was in that moment when you had found a ball and then you had to decide, in a split second, whether to surrender it or ditch it. It never failed to start up a surge of adrenaline.

I remember well my first encounter with a shagger. By the age of 13 or 14 I had an ambivalent role at the park: too old to be a mere scrambler, a ball surrenderer, and too young to be a shagger. And I was no wimp, and the shaggers knew it. One night I was sitting on a favorite limb, outside the right-field foul line, watching the game. The batter hit a high foul ball my way and I heard Hastings' "Creeeeek!" I lost the ball a moment, but then it crashed through the branches over my head, barely missing me, and splashed in the creek. I slid down the trunk, rolled up my pantlegs to my knees and waded in, scooped up the floating ball, scrambled up the far bank and started sprinting for the railroad tracks. I knew the scoreboard shagger saw it all; for the first time I was openly defying him. I wasn't looking back but I heard him on his side of the creek: "Evans I'll kick your ass!"

I kept running. Across the highway over the ditch into the weeds, onto the tracks. It was dusk, I could still see fairly well, so I was taking the shortcut home that would go around the rat pond and up the steps of the bluff onto Wall Street. When I had plenty of distance between myself and the park, I slowed down and looked back. A shagger was after me, Hastings' right-hand man, and then I saw Hastings on the roof, pointing at us, and others watching too.

By the time I got to the rat pond I could hear the guy behind me, since by then the noise of the ball park had diminished. The long intervals of his steps, the hard huffing told me he was running all out. But all I had to do was keep running. I was fast enough. I slowed down on the narrow path that went around the pond; the path was muddy from a recent rain. Just as I was about to clear the pond by jumping up onto the next set of

8

railroad tracks above it, I saw a rat. It was one of the biggest rats I'd ever seen. I couldn't go around it because of the water on one side, and the mounds of rubbish which might have more rats in them, on the other side. Rats scared me, even when I was not alone. I'd seen people attacked when they tried to corner them, here and in the sewer under Wall Street, the rats charging with fierce squeaks. The fact that I had stolen a baseball—a brand new one at that—increased my fear by adding guilt to it. This rat, maybe, had been laying for me? The Rat of Guilt?

So there I was, crouched, frozen, stopped by a staring rat, with a shagger bearing down on me. I cocked the ball, my only weapon, and aimed for the face. I brought it down as hard as I could into the rat's back just behind the neck. The ball stuck like the apple in Greger Sampsa's side in Kafka's story. The rat squeaked once, and started to die. I looked closely at its eyes. Glass beads, crayfish eyes, bulging. The same eyes I had seen in the rat traps my father used to set in the basement of our acreage house many years before. The same hideous bubble of blood growing at the edge of the mouth.

I didn't want the ball now; I leaped over the rat onto the bank and headed for the steps. When I got to the first landing I stopped and looked back. The shagger had evidently found his ball because he was walking back to the park. I imagined him digging it out of the rat's back and wiping it off on his pantlegs to make it look new again for Hastings.

The incident changed my role at the ball park. I never again felt like I might be in line for a shagging job. The shagger didn't kick my ass. He had only been bluffing. But after all, Hastings had gotten his ball back, which was the main thing.

Now I had some leeway. I wouldn't from then on openly taunt the shaggers, and yet they knew I wouldn't hesitate to take game balls if I got the chance. The price of my relative freedom to disdain the shaggers' authority was their lack of interest in me. No more sitting on the scoreboard. No more running the ball up to Hastings on the roof when the floating shagger was too busy. But it wasn't a bad price.

Watching the ball game and chasing after balls weren't the only recreations at the Soos' park. There were special nights, like Shrine Night sponsored by the Sioux City Shriners, with various contests and acts. I was in an ice-cream eating contest once, which took place near the pitcher's mound. Eight or ten of us kids were lined up and handed an ice-cream spoon and a quart of vanilla ice cream apiece. When the voice on the P.A. system said go, we were to see who could down the most in three minutes. The crowd laughed hysterically but we were gluttons in earnest. I won, and nearly froze my stomach.

The great pitcher Dizzy Dean was invited to town one day for a Shrine game. Dean had been drinking heavily all day. Obviously feeling loose, he stepped up to the plate before a packed-in crowd, somebody threw him a pitch at batting-practice speed and Dean clobbered the ball over the center field fence, a hell of a poke for anybody.

There was a man billed as "the clown prince of baseball," an ex-player evidently, who would put on a show before games. Dressed in a baseball suit, with a clown's face, he would shoot a ball almost straight up out of a cannon at home plate, get in his jeep and roar into center field where the ball—shot so high you could have taken a coffee break under it—was coming down. He would circle, do figure eights, zig zag, stand up in the seat, steer sitting backwards or with his feet and, at the last second drive under the ball and reach out and snag it in his oversized catcher's mitt. I never saw him miss. He was amazing.

We invented our own recreations too, for instance, peeking at the women. One way was to walk under the bleachers or grandstand pretending, official faced, to be looking for a dropped billfold or set of keys, and then simply look up under the dresses and slips. There was a joke among us that always got raging laughs. Someone would say:

"Ever read the book, *Under the Grandstand,* by Seymour Butt?" It wasn't until years later that I realized that "Seymour" was the name of a person; at the time I thought it was spelled "See More," since that's what it sounded like.

The joke was all the more delicious because we could raunch it up by changing the end of it.

"*Under the Grandstand,* by Seymour Pussy?"

"*Under the Grandstand,* by Seymour Ass?" And so on.

The other way of watching the women was even more interesting. Some clever boys, in the daytime when nobody was around, had drilled a couple of holes in the wall of the women's restroom. Usually the buses were parked just outside the back of the restroom, and the area was not well lighted, so we had a secret place for viewing. But we had to be careful. If we were caught we'd be kicked out, maybe for good. We took turns being a sentry, and took turns peering through the holes. The bigger you were the longer you got to look, and the better was the object for your eyeball. Sometimes we'd make such a racket arguing over whose turn it was to look, that the woman inside heard us. She would either stuff the hole with tissue or leave and report us to the management, or both. Eventually there were so many complaints that the management boarded up the holes and alerted the bus drivers, some of whom had themselves been peekers, to report any funny business.

I have two unerasable images from that eyeballing. One is a woman struggling out of a girdle so tight I thought it was her skin. The other is a pair of white panties with blue stripes. They belonged to a player's wife, a beautiful woman I could never again look at without being both embarrassed and agitated.

4

The names. Thirty years away, the names are still an enchantment to me. To say out loud—to write down. Eddie Bressoud, Bill White, Ernie Yellen, Billy Pavlick, Mario Picone, Ray Johnson. Of all the names I once knew over the several summers of games I went to, so few come back to me, and yet those few blaze in my memory.

Bressoud, White, and Picone were the only ones on my remembered list who made it to the majors, and Bressoud and White distinguished themselves, especially White, one of the few Blacks who played for the Soos. Maybe it's mostly because

11

they made it big that I remember their names so readily. I have no image of White, though I'm sure I saw him play. He played one year with the Soos, and then was called up. One fact sticks: that he long-jumped 24 feet in high school. That may be legend, like being told by old timers (as I have been) that a poor kid named Willie Mays once hitch-hiked to Sioux City, tried out for the team, and wasn't quite good enough. Only recently did I hear the real story, which is not what the legend says. During the 1949 or 1950 season somebody in the New York Giants' front office in New York (the Soos were a Giant farm club) called the brass in the Sioux City front office and asked if they wanted a kid still in high school in Alabama, a black kid destined to be a major leaguer. His name was Mays, they had already signed him up, and the Giants thought he was ready for Class A. The only problem, as far as the Soos were concerned, was the color of his skin. Very few teams in the early 50s were ready to take black players, and Sioux City was not about to start anything.

Willie Mays then bypassed class A, went directly to the Minneapolis triple-A club, tore up the league with a .477 batting average, and soon was called up to New York City. The rest, as everybody knows, is baseball history.

I remember Bressoud, a true natural. He broke in with the Soos and quickly became a star shortstop at the age of 16 or 17. I can still see him moving, nifty as a cat, snagging hot grounders with unbelievable ease. In his floppy uniform, with his boyish face, he might have been mistaken for the bat boy.

For me, the name Billy Pavlick is magical. He too was young, an outfielder with a tremendous throwing arm, a good clutch hitter, and very popular with the crowd. Sometimes before a game several outfielders would get together in deep right center near the scoreboard and make bets on who could throw a ball the farthest. They took turns throwing toward the grandstand. I once saw Pavlick actually throw a ball over the grandstand roof. His catapult arm was his main talent. You heard the name Pavlick so often around the ball park that you assumed he would one day be a big leaguer.

He did play briefly in double A, but was paralyzed when he fell off a ladder while painting. His brief life as a ball player reminds me of A. E. Housman's famous poem, "To an

Athlete Dying Young,'' in which the poet celebrates the death of a young runner, whom he calls a ''smart lad, to slip betimes away/From fields where glory does not stay,'' and opposes him to those athletes who have sadly outlived their playing days, ''Runners whom renown outran/And the name died before the man.''

I have a clear memory of Ernie Yellen, a catcher. Tall, ghostly pale, reserved, one cheek packed with tobacco, Yellen had the peculiar habit of cocking and flicking his wrist once or twice before he released the ball. I imitated him as a catcher in my sophomore year in high school, but I could never get that sudden flick just before I released the ball. It was all show when I did it; it seemed natural for Yellen, though it must have cost him a split-second in his pegs on attempted steals. He was one of those ''regulars'' who stayed on year after year and was never good enough to play above Class A.

Mario Picone. Black hair, handsome, a flashy pitcher with good speed. He was the kind that the women—perfumed and high-heeled and lovely—not only came to watch but to seek out after the game for an autograph, a date, a diamond, marriage, a family.

Ray Johnson was my favorite. He was a center fielder, extremely fast. He even *looked* fast. About five-ten, he had a piston-shaped body, a small, greyhound head with a thick jaw, a crewcut with a pronounced whorl in front, and legs that seemed too heavy for his body. His calves and thighs were immense. He hit first in the line-up because he was a good bunter and base stealer. He liked the ball high over the plate, almost eye-level. He rarely hit popups. He hit sizzling line drives that carried all the way to the fence, often striking it near the top. Everybody loved to see him run. He could beat out routine grounders for singles if the ball was not sharply fielded and thrown. He could stretch singles into doubles, doubles into triples, triples into inside-the-park homeruns. He would hit the ball, say, deep into the right-center gap, and go flying around the bases, legs blurring, arms pumping wildly.

Johnson had one flaw that was to keep him from rising. He had stiff wrists, and so he couldn't get around well on the ball. He looked like a man swinging a board. The coaches worked with him constantly in batting practice, but he never found a natural swing.

17

His throwing arm was sometimes erratic too. Once I saw him field a high-bouncing single on one bounce, and with a man rounding third to try to score, he rocked into his throw with plausible grace and fired the ball almost directly into the ground! It wasn't that Johnson had trouble getting *to* the ball or catching it. I saw him make some wonderful back-handed grabs at full speed and some wonderful throws; but his arm, though strong, was inconsistent.

I've always thought it was Johnson's peculiar fate to have been blessed with so much speed that when it came to other talents he had to come up short somewhere. One great gift balanced by one great flaw. Yet if baseball was played like football—defense and offense—he might well have been a major league outfielder.

He was not one of the most accessible players on the team, but he was decent if somewhat standoffish. He did talk and joke with us boys. But one night everything changed, as far as he and I were concerned. What happened between us has a brief history.

In the spring of 1953, shortly after the Missouri River flood waters subsided, I was scrounging around the ball park with a couple of friends, looking for anything useful. Outside the club house I found a lump of mud in the shape of a fielder's glove.

I took it home and over a period of several weeks fixed it pocket-down on a fence post in my backyard and pounded out the mud and water with a bat and the heel of my hand, and let the glove dry in the sun. I spent hours on it, squeezing, pounding, re-shaping it. Finally it was dry enough and I oiled it, constantly pounding the pocket, forcing it back into shape. It had a few cracks and was still soggy deep inside the fingers for weeks, but I had restored it pretty much to its original condition before the flood. Gradually, as the wrist band dried, I found a name on it: ''Ray Johnson.'' I scratched out the name and wrote in my own. It was mine.

By the middle of the baseball season I had sold the glove for five dollars to a friend named Dale Nickolson. I loved that glove but felt slightly guilty keeping it, and the money was too good to turn down. I had never had the nerve to take the glove to the games because Johnson might see it and claim it. I might even be accused of stealing. But Nickolson had had no such fears. He of course could act innocent and say that he bought the glove from me, which was true.

One night between games of a double header, Ray Johnson walked by Nickolson and me and noticed the glove. He stopped.

"Where'd you get that glove?" he said.

My legs went weak. Dale didn't hesitate; he pointed at me. "From him," he said.

"Can I see it?" Johnson asked, and Nickolson handed it to him. He put it on, pounded the pocket a few times, then unbuttoned the wrist band and held the glove close to his eyes. He showed it to us.

"See this?" he said. There was a trace of hostility in his voice. I saw it: the name "Ray Johnson" printed neatly — secretly — in blue ink in a little circle around the steel wrist-band button. What could I say? I who had scratched out "Ray Johnson" and printed "Dave Evans" in its place; I who had sold the glove — whose glove? — to a friend who had scratched out "Dave Evans" and printed "Dale Nickolson" in bold letters on the thumb? Johnson asked me where I got it, and I told him about finding it after the flood, about restoring it on my fence post. He seemed surprised to see it in such good shape. He kept pounding the pocket, turning the glove over, pounding it, feeling it. I knew he wasn't pleased that I'd taken the glove in the first place, and yet he was happy to see it again.

He asked Nickolson if he could use it in the second game, Nickolson obliged, and he walked off, pounding the pocket. I watched him closely in the outfield. He was like a 10-year old kid, pampering that glove as if it was a birthday gift. After the game he bought it back from Nickolson for ten dollars. From then on I more or less avoided Johnson's eye, and he treated me with what H.L. Mencken called a "freezing courtesy."

5

Why does one man, Ray Johnson, dominate my memories of the Soos? The ball glove incident is one reason, no doubt. But there is another, more fundamental reason, which I discovered only after I began to dig through my past: Johnson and I are alike. It's not simply that out of admiration I've unconsciously or consciously tried to emulate him. It's almost as if, through memory, which I now know is not static but dynamic and creative, Ray Johnson and I have melded into one person.

I too had powerful legs and the gift of speed. I too can be standoffish and arrogant, even when I seem friendly. One habit of the 50s, at least in Sioux City among those I grew up with, was to put all your fragile eggs in one fragile basket. Maybe it was a survival strategy we got from our fathers who had picked it up out of the depression. The prescription: *take that one talent or skill or connection or label that says who you are, and apply it.*

By the age of 14 I had discovered a strategy that worked for me: speed, which, my coaches used to say, makes up for a lot of mistakes. I had run easily inside a river of headlights, had actually outrun cars on electric legs of fear up Wall Street. Later, in high school I stretched out for long, off-tackle touchdowns, and, like Ray Johnson, ran down fly balls, beat out bunts, stole bases. And when I graduated I was handed a football scholarship, a chance for an education on the promise of pure speed; but I found out after one season that speed wasn't everything. There were also blocking and tackling and guts. There were also others — including a kid with a butch haircut from Chicago who ran the hundred in 9.7 — who were faster or just as fast as I was.

I depended mainly on that one thing, but that one thing failed to sustain me. All I could do then, with that new knowledge, was fail all the more completely. So I did. Openly, honestly, deliberately, adamantly, wholesomely — I refused to perform, to attempt other strategies, until that moment when, coming home after a game on a team bus from Vermillion, South Dakota to Sioux Falls, South Dakota, the words of the coach up front busted through the dark, words I knew would be coming sooner or later, like a baseball fired at my face: EVANS YOU'RE THROUGH!

And so I was, with the pure speed thing.

The Place Of Your Dream

My mother tells me that when I was as young as two I used to sit alone in our backyard on the Wall Street bluff above the railroad tracks, and watch trains for hours. I don't remember it but it's easy to believe because we moved to another house on that same bluff when I was seven, and I often watched trains, day or night, either from the bluff or from the creosote-stained steps running down it. A couple of nights a week a passenger train went by with its windows lighted, many of them with a profile of a face. The train clicked cleanly through the dark, and if there was a moon the wheels and rails shone like beaten nickels. Sitting there alone, I often wondered what the travelers — separate profiles in separate windows — were thinking.

The image of trains seen from a bluff has stayed with me, a gift of memory. My father died when I was 23, and for at least a decade no day went by without him dominating my thoughts. Dead, he was as real to me as he had been when living. One night in my 30s I dreamed I was a boy again, watching a night train from that same bluff. Suddenly I saw his face repeated in each lighted window, the face of a man passing from one kind of darkness into another. High above him, I waved, and it seemed like I was waving at him for the last time.

My dream didn't erase my father from my thoughts, but perhaps subconsciously it showed me that I *could* live without him — as all sons must learn so that we can be fathers.

I am speaking of heights more than of fathers, though the two tend to go together.

Getting up on a high place and enjoying a panoramic view is more than a matter of vision. Not long ago, when the Foshay Tower in Minneapolis was that city's tallest building, I was on its observation floor 55 stories up, looking out on the city. I

21

turned around and saw an obese, blind, American Indian woman helped out of an elevator by another woman, no doubt her friend. The two made their way to the safety fence at the edge of the roof. The blind woman paused, faced the steep wind like the rest of us, smiled, and said with perfect clarity:

"I've always wanted to see Minneapolis from this height."

Of course she couldn't have meant the word "see" literally. What she meant, I believe, had something to do with being up high over a landscape, of having a perspective and vantage point she couldn't have on the ground. In a word, having some *control*.

The desire to get up high and the satisfaction we feel when we can *take in* so much beneath us, must be part of our biological inheritance. Almost all vertebrates, when challenged, inflate to make themselves look bigger and taller. When they lose a fight or argument they deflate and slink around with an averted eye, and appease the winners. When they win they strut, tall and confident.

We humans are no different, but we turn the biology into words that parallel our actions. We too get our hackles and our hair up. We put lifts in our shoes to appear more formidable, get pumped up for contests, vie for the tallest trophies and the position of top dog. We look up to our parents. We shoulder responsibilities as well as heroes, dead or living. We elevate our gods to the sky, and heavens to aspire up to. We bow and scrape to superiors and overlords, those over us. Or, as high brows, we raise our supercilious eyebrows and snub low brows, inferiors and underlings. We hold summit conferences, build capitols on hills for our chiefs (heads or higher-ups), who step up to power or step down out of it. We feel down or downcast or low when things go badly, high or up when they go well.

Shakespeare expressed the biology beautifully in his portrait of the great Caesar:

> Why, man, he doth bestride the narrow world
> Like a Colossus, and we petty men
> Walk under his huge legs and peep about
> To find ourselves dishonorable graves.

22

A recent American writer named William Gass expressed the same thing in 20th century fashion: "I want to rise so high that when I shit I won't miss anybody."

I have something to celebrate. I was born on a bluff in a town whose origin was dreamed from a bluff. The story of Sioux City, Iowa is the story of bluffs and hills and rivers. In the late 1840s — if one can believe his journal — a man named Bruguier, a fur trader friendly with Sioux Indians in the area, married Chief War Eagle's daughter. One night, while living up the Missouri, Bruguier was restless and couldn't sleep. He dreamed that he saw a place where three rivers came together within a few miles, and bluffs and trees — all of which he had never seen before. When he awakened, his dream troubled him, and he told his father-in-law about it. War Eagle recognized the place as Bruguier described it, and said, "I will take you there."

The two came down the river, and at the mouth of the Sioux (after which Sioux City was eventually named) War Eagle said, "This is the place of your dream. Here can be a great camp."

The third river of the dream was the Floyd River, named after Seargent Floyd, the only man to die on the Lewis and Clark Expedition. Clark wrote in his original journal:

> Serjeant Floyd is taken verry bad all at once with a Biliose Chorlick we attempt to reliev him without success as yet, he gets worse and we are much allarmed at his situation, all attention to him . . . Died with a great deel of composure, before his death he said to me 'I am going away I want you to write me a letter' — We buried him on the top of the bluff ½ mile below a small river to which he gave his name, he was buried with the Honors of War much lamented, a seeder post with the Name Sergt. C. Floyd died here 20th of August 1804 was fixed at the head of his grave — This man at all times gave us proofs of his firmness and Determined resolution to doe service to his countrey and honor to himself after paying all the honor to our Deceased brother we camped in the mouth of floyd's river about 30 yards wide, a butifull evening.

In 1832 the painter George Catlin came up the river in the steamboat Yellowstone, paused at "Floyd's Grave" long enough to paint it (as did Karl Bodmer a year later), and wrote of the view:

> I several times ascended it and sat and contemplated the solitude and stillness of this tenanted mound; and beheld from its top the windings infinite of the Missouri . . . its thousand hills and domes of green vanishing into blue in the distance . . .

In 1900, a 100-foot obelisk with a sharp, pyramidal point was erected on that same bluff. It is called Floyd's Monument.

24

NATIONAL HISTORIC SITE
FLOYD
MONUMENT

   As a boy, some friends and I made swords out of laths and
climbed that bluff and others along the Missouri, pretending
to be in the "Lewis and Clark Exploration." Always our goal
was to get up high enough to cup a hand over our eyes and look
down at the glittering river. I'm not sure if it ever occurred to
us that Lewis and Clark had done their traveling in *boats*—we
imagined them cutting trails through trees and over hills,
doing Indians in, exploring always on foot.

   My hometown—a place of hills and rivers in the grassy
center of the prairie—had many heights for a growing boy to

25

see from. (I was lucky: my parents gave me almost total freedom to run and play. Mine was such a physical boyhood that I can barely remember the inside of the three houses I lived in before my high school years.)

In my early teens I sometimes stopped at the public library on Saturday mornings on the way to the YMCA, not for books but to hear records of poetry readings. That was my first awakening to poetry (though not to other literature), and it was no accident that the very first poem that I couldn't help memorizing was "Dover Beach" by Mathew Arnold — a poem whose words are spoken from a bluff above the sea. I didn't understand every word but I caught the music from those opening lines:

> The sea is calm tonight,
> The tide is full, the moon lies fair
> Upon the straits — on the French coast the light
> Gleams and is gone, the cliffs of England stand,
> Glimmering and vast, out in the tranquil bay.
> Come to the window, sweet is the night air.

These lines and images made sense to me, I know now, because I too had looked down from bluffs — had seen how moonlight strikes water or land, how "the light gleams and is gone"; had heard the roar of, if not the sea, the Missouri and the trains. I could never get enough of the poem. I can still recite it. When I began to write poems a decade or so later I used my middle name Allan because the name of the reader of "Dover Beach" was David Allen.

Neither was it an accident that the first "recent" poem by an American that got to me (not counting Carl Sandburg) was "In the Tree House at Night" by James Dickey, which begins:

> And now the green household is dark,
> The half-moon completely is shining
> On the earth-lighted tops of the trees . . .

I too had had a tree house as a boy; I too had climbed the "sprained, comic rungs of the ladder," where I came out "at last over lakes/of leaves, of fields disencumbered of earth."

26

On the Wall Street bluff, between our brick house and the house at the top of the hill (owned by a family named Hillsinger), was a weedy vacant lot with a tall tree in it. It was the tree that Ronnie Tolar fell out of one night and broke his left arm in the same place for the third time. My cross-eyed friend, Dale Jimeson, had been watching Ronnie from the ground with a flashlight. When I asked him what he did when Ronnie fell, he said: "I followed him down with my flashlight."

That was the same tree I used to climb just to get away. I climbed up to near the giddy top branches, clothespinned my legs in a favorite crotch so I was half-standing, half-sitting, and swayed and watched and thought. And sometimes sang. Once I swayed and boomed out the words of "On Top of Old Smokey" over and over.

And then one summer I had a lofty experience on a pile of sand.

I was playing hide-and-seek with two friends at a gravel company below the railroad bluff. It was my turn to hide, so I climbed to the top of a pyramid of sand, and was watching my friends some 30 feet below, who were looking for me. They walked by between some railroad tracks, not thinking to look up (they could have easily seen me if they had).

I closed my eyes and felt my heart, which was still racing from the climb, but more than that, going wild with a secret excitement. Just then, strangely, I saw myself as a man 20 or 30 years away. High up on that sun-baked sand, I knew that some day, in whatever distant place I was living, I would remember — exactly — *that* secret moment, *that* wild heartbeat.

*   *   *

For the last 15 years I've lived in a flat town in a flat part of South Dakota. I do have my second-story bedroom window to look out of, and I enjoy the way moonlight plays on the top of my apple tree in the backyard, and the way the streetlight beyond the alley blinks through the elms.

But I miss the hills and rivers, especially the glittering Missouri in the spring. Whenever I travel, my habit is to get up high and look down. Or if I'm driving on Interstate 29 to

Sioux City, 150 miles away, there is one long hill near Vermillion that I need to get over so that the wide expanse of the Missouri Valley with its dark, shaggy bluffs can open up for me. The moment I get to the peak of that hill and look down is the moment I know I am home.

"Fear Is What Quickens Me"

THINGS IN THE DARK

I've always been afraid of the dark, and I've always enjoyed my fear. Even now in my 40s, sometimes if I'm in my basement office at night I'll deliberately turn out all the lights and *feel* my way through the furnace room and up the stairs. The fear is increased in this case because I might bump my head on something I can't see. I go stooped and wide-eyed, waving my hands in front of me to clear a path. I keep expecting things to lurch out from under the stairs or from behind the furnace. A face, an eye, a hand — glowing. I listen for low, throaty growls. Once I get a foot on the steps I leap three or four at a time on panicky legs, the athlete pheonixed from a middle-aged body. Up, up I go, and crash through the door into the kitchen, the light.

Basements make me nervous anyway. My memory is too vivid. When I was a boy my father used to tell us kids a story that went like this: a family is eating supper, and the father tells one of his boys to go down to the basement and get some more butter. The boy goes down the stairs and is suddenly confronted by a huge man who grabs him and tells him he won't harm him if he'll go back up and send his father down — on the pretense that the boy can't find the butter. (I forget why the man prefers the father, if I ever did know why — it sounds like a version of the "Three Billy Goats Gruff.") The boy goes upstairs and tells his father about the man he saw, and so the father must go down himself. And so he does (my father's face and voice turned grim when he got to this part):

"One step. . . Two step. . . Three step. . . Four step. . . Five step. . ." (all the way down to the bottom step like this). . . "Ten step — GOTTCHA!"

The dramatic build-up itself—the descent into the basement in such simple, slow-paced inevitable words—my father's exaggerated tone as he told it, were enough to make the hair on my neck stand up. But the crescendo always frightened me to the center of my bones. I loved to have him tell the story and yet it scared the hell out of me.

In the early 50s, in winter, my two brothers and some friends and I used to block up our basement windows with cardboard or dark paper, turn out the lights and play Capture the Flag in complete darkness. The object of the game was to place two "flags" (rags, handkerchiefs) in spots agreed on beforehand, on either side of the basement, which we had divided into two equal-sized territories, one for each team. Say there were three on a side. One would hang around the flag and protect it from invaders (though the rule said he had to be at least 10-15 feet from the flag so the invader could have access). The other two would sneak across the line and try to steal the flag. Whenever somebody got caught outside his territory he was taken hostage. Whenever somebody got a flag and was able to get back across the line without being caught, the game was over, his team won, and the lights were turned on.

The game was most fun in the dark because we couldn't see the enemy—we might bump into him any second. We didn't dare say anything either, or make a noise—that would give us away. So on hands and knees, barely breathing, we crept through the dark on the cool cement floor, often beneath wet clothes hanging from plastic clotheslines, toward the flag. It was best to move a few feet at a time, then stop and listen, then move again. (I didn't like guarding the flag, and usually begged off that job if we were taking turns. I never did like defense. It's too serious, too altruistic, too static for me. I'm strictly an offensive player; I have to be a performer, on my own, extending myself, eluding opponents.)

I was especially tense in those moments just after I'd found the flag, stuffed it in my back pocket, and was on my way back to safety. Now I had a double pressure on me: to be caught would be to lose not only personally but also for my team. Always close to panic, I was even more nimble and alert.

The excitement I felt in that basement—the gut excitement

of being stealthy, of crawling around in enemy territory in darkness as black as a cave — is impossible to describe. I'm convinced that the feeling is so fundamental, biological and hormonal as to be beyond words.

But it must have something to do with the risk involved in trying to steal an item of high value from someone. Capturing the flag may have been the symbolic equivalent of castration, I don't know. I do know that, in real life there is no emptier, more helpless feeling — except what follows the death of someone close — than being ripped off.

The risk-taking; the dangerous proximity to the enemy, whose invisible face might be close enough to your own invisible face to actually breathe into it; the urge to scream out and give yourself away because the tension was too much for you; the need to be as silent as an Apache stealing horses — all this was unbelieveably fun and scary at the same time.

And all of us felt it together. (Probably the main reason for playing in the dark was to get high on the fear.) Someone would flick on the lights when a game was over, and we'd freeze in place. We expressed ourselves in wild bursts of words, slapped our thighs, guffawed, looked around — spotted our enemy, saw how close we were to the flag or to being caught. "I *knew* it was you," someone would say, or "Another 10 seconds I would've had the flag!" We could hardly contain ourselves, and we were always eager for another go-round. It was the explosive joy of young males in a group, and there's nothing quite like it, except orgasmic release.

Monster movies were another source of fear. As a boy I begged my older brother to take me to see *Frankenstein* and all the others, but what I actually saw of the movies was not often much, since I spent most of the time down behind the seat in front of me. (I wonder if some of my impatience with most plots of movies and novels isn't traceable to this early movie-watching. What interests me are glimpses, confrontations — scenes, poems, and short stories rather than whole movies or novels.) Half crying, my hands clamped on my ears, I'd peek over the seat for glimpses of the gore. Without the redundant music and sound effects, the horror was almost tolerable.

31

Once, in the old Orpheum theatre when *The Thing* was playing (with James Arness as the monster from outer space) I was on my way to the lobby and the bathroom, just as a cool arctic scientist in a white frock was lifting the lid—slowly, cautiously—of a large box, hoping (not hoping?) to find some evidence of The Thing's bloodlust. With the music rising, I was about half way up the aisle, knowing something bad was about to happen. I looked back—caught between my seat and the lobby—the music crescendoed and there it was: a dead dog in the box. Fear stuck in my spine like a knife, I bolted the rest of the way and crashed through the double-swinging doors while faces in the seats laughed at me. After I came back from the bathroom and had recovered my reason, I was embarrassed, and took the other aisle back to my seat, the long way around, to avoid the faces.

For me, the scariest monsters were those with both human and non-human traits: The Wolfman, Dracula, The Thing, The Creature from the Black Lagoon, The Mummy. The strictly non-human species didn't affect me nearly as much: blobs, invisible "forces," berserk gorillas, flying saucers with long goose-necks, giant cats and spiders. One reason these things didn't release real fear in me, I suppose, is that they lacked human emotion and an evil intention. After all, machines and animals don't *consciously* set out to do evil to others. But if Lugosi's Dracula or Karloff's Frankenstein or Mummy weren't at any given moment intent on destroying people, it didn't take much to provoke them. And once on your trail there was no turning them around.

These creatures usually had one or two traits that made them memorably horrible: Frankenstein with his angry, beastial snarl; The Wolfman with his shifty, lickerish eyes and animated movements; Dracula with his black, reptilian stare; The Creature from the Black Lagoon with his shark-like speed underwater; The Mummy with his bandaged muteness.

But it was their relentlessness that gripped me. They kept coming, through fire, bombs, electricity, bullets, chain nets, gas; they kept coming. They wouldn't let up until they had found you and torn your head from your shoulders. Always a little paranoid, I identified easily with the pursued, never the pursuer. It was *my* head the monsters were after.

Karloff's Frankenstein's monster was one of my favorites. He didn't walk so much as teeter like The Tin Man, stiff-arming and snarling as he went. Since his neck had a bolt stuck through it, and his seamed, square head couldn't turn, his mien was always straight ahead and headlong. He could affect a smile, as if thinking, with Shakespeare's Richard, "I can smile, and murder whilst I smile, and cry content to that which grieves my heart." He must have realized he had the wrong brain, the extra, criminal chromosome, and so he was, like Richard, a griever, but he was no schemer. He was more spontaneous and violent, like Faulkner's pissed-off barn burner who walks around with a "machine-like deliberation."

There is one Frankenstein scene I'll never forget. The monster has escaped his maker and is off on a tangent, in some woods, crashing through branches and small trees, when he breaks out into the open by spreading the foliage like curtains, and sees a little girl in a pretty dress, sitting on the bank of a river. She is picking flowers and tossing them into the water and watching them float on the current. The monster approaches, curious, and the girl is not afraid of him but rather invites him, wordlessly, to join in. He sits down beside her, half-smiling, and watches the flowers floating away. The two are happy. The camera zooms in on a few flowers on the water, and the scene fades out.

Suddenly, in the next scene a man, presumably the girl's father, is carrying her limp body into the village, his face gray and blank.

What made the sequence so intriguing and yet horrifying to me was not the drowning of the girl by the monster. That was to be expected. It was the extreme contrast between the pleasant—girl and monster recreating together in a touching scene—and the opposite of the pleasant—murder—which is not explicit but implied. But mostly it was the symbolic *connection* the monster made between the girl and the flowers. So: did he really want to kill her, or did he simply want to see if she too, like the other flowers, could float on the water? The disinterestedness of the evil jolted me. I had just witnessed the poetry of horror.

I could never get enough of the werewolf's painful metamorphosis, especially Lon Chaney Jr.'s. The next day after a Wolfman movie I'd stare into the bathroom mirror and try for that layered, cosmetic sequence. I imagined the moon above, and those dark rags of clouds scudding across it in fast motion (or was the moon itself moving, and not the clouds?). The moon was changing too, as my face would. Now dark, now bright, now dark, now shining like a silver dollar stuck in the sky. I raised my upper lip, flashed my teeth, growled, at myself, at the world; predicted bloody homicide for gangs of men with torches hounding me into the hills, toward the Missouri, a cave on the bluffs, maybe. I was ready for anything my face could make me do. I felt for hair along my cheeks. I shifted my look back and forth, caught the white edge of perversion. I closed my eyes, expecting, when I opened them again, to see the spittled canines, the hair, the face of self-pity of the man who couldn't help it.

But I could help it. My eyes were too honest and too blue; I couldn't get them to go for the wolf. I tried and tried, but I was still Dave Evans.

THE OLD MAN

There were real people who scared me too. For instance, the senile grandfather of a good friend who lived up the street on the edge of the bluff overlooking the railroad and streetcar tracks. This old man, not quite decrepit enough to be bedridden and yet too feeble to read or hold a conversation (he only mumbled), would sit, day after day, in a wheelchair next to his bed in his tiny bedroom, mostly staring with eyes of isinglass, and fumbling with his knobby fingers. He had that toothless, dry, seamed, puckered, fist-face aspect of the hopelessly old.

I'd sometimes stay overnight with my friend, which meant that I had to pass through the man's room to get to the bathroom, and he was always there, a hazard, near the bathroom door, staring, waiting—for what?

I'd step through the door heading for the bathroom and his look would change when he saw me: a look, say, of a rowdy boy watching a cat being flung around by its tail—a look that wants a piece of the action. I approached him with caution, faking confidence, and sometimes when I was passing him

34

he'd suddenly reach out and grab at my arm. He usually meant only to startle me, but once his hand did clamp on my wrist like a vice and I had to jerk free. He liked seeing me wince, and made a noice that was a half-cough, half-laugh.

Coming back from the bathroom was no problem, since the old man's attention span was so short that he forgot I existed once I was out of sight. Also, he was facing the opposite way, so I could quickly slip by him. But when I got to the bedroom door and looked back at him, he had that same mischievious expression on his face.

Even now, decades later, whenever I'm confronted with a situation in which I know I'll have to suffer some pain before I can get to something pleasurable, the old man's image often comes to me. He is a symbol for that specific kind of tension. For him, then, I must have represented a spark, or a curlicue cut across the vague midnight of old age.

THE JUNKMAN

There was a deaf and dumb junk dealer in our neighborhood, a wiry, heron-eyed, small-headed man who always wore a greasy black seed hat. We boys called him Deefy. He pulled his two-wheeled junk cart up and down our cindered alleys looking for anything he could sell, trade or hock. Useful, fabulous junk: bike tires and frames and chains, lamps, bathroom cabinets, mattresses, wagon tongues, hubcaps, overstuffed or folding chairs, frying pans, flashlights, picture frames (empty or otherwise), vacuum cleaners, mirrors, doors, shingles, rakes, hoes, sinks, bird baths, saws, comic books. He hoarded everything.

We could hear the wheels of his cart crunching the cinders a block away. We loved to follow him, at a safe distance, and mock him and taunt him with insane gestures and words, especially behind his back. He knew the best way of handling us was to keep plodding straight ahead as if everything was normal; the less commotion the better. From a quarter of a block away we'd throw rocks *toward* him, never quite *at* him, but sometimes they'd *whang* off the back of his cart and he'd feel the vibration and suddenly stop. The cart handles would shoot up, he'd whirl around and nail us with an eye and scream an eerie, wild scream that scattered us like shotgunned rats down the alley, over yards, across streets, howling for joy. To him, his voice must have felt like a violent expulsion of air; to us, it was the rending of steel.

Sometimes we'd follow his bobbing seed hat all the way to his house—almost a shack—a block and a half down the street from my house, where he lived with his deaf and dumb wife. (They had a son our age, with normal hearing and speech, who lived with relatives.) There he'd lock up his loaded cart inside a wooden gate and go in, ignoring us more. So our rocks thudded on his plywood windows, on his front door. Or, if one of us was brave enough we'd sneak up and "ring" his doorbell, which was a light in his front room, and run back to the others, crouched behind some bushes. Tense and light-footed, we waited for the door to explode its hinges. He must have hated and feared us for our taunting, our rocks, our constant pestering that interrupted his meagre yet serious attempts at making a living. I think he would have loved to get his hands on just one of us for a lesson. But he never came out.

My fear of the junkman was not simply a piece of neighborhood mythology. It was more like xenophobia: deep and irrational. I had dreams of him chasing me down alleys, my legs and arms pumping in slow motion, his quick, jerky steps and wild grunts growing louder and louder behind me. Awake or asleep, I imagined him catching me with his wiry arms, squeezing my neck, screwing his thumbs in my eyes, screaming in my face like a maniac.

And then one night something happened that not even a dream could dream up.

I had been to a monster movie with a couple of friends and was jogging the three blocks home from where the bus had let me off. My friends had gone their own ways, I had only streetlights for company. My habit after dark, whether I'd been to a monster movie or not, was to avoid alleys, but this night I decided to push my fear a little. When I got to Strongin's grocery store, a block east of my house, I had three options: straight up the alley; around the block to the south, which would take me by the junkman's house—even though he'd no doubt be in bed (I'd never seen him out at night), I didn't like passing his house; and around the block to the north.

36

I decided on the shortest route and took off up the alley. Running full speed at night was dangerous because I couldn't hear anybody or anything above the sound of my footsteps, and yet I was too scared to slow down and listen. I was at top speed when I hit the intersection half way home, just as the junkman and his cart appeared and met me exactly in the center of the alley—we couldn't have timed the meeting better! At first I was more surprised than scared. Not missing a stride I veered sharply—a butterfly caught in a sudden blast of wind—nearly bumping the cart going around it, and continued my straight line home. The junkman had had even less time to react, since he was looking the other way. When he saw me he skidded, his cart handles flew up and he grunted, startled. I got to the end of the alley, took a rounded left, my momentum carrying me out into the street, and when I got to my house I jumped over the picket fence and was gone.

After that night I never again mocked the junkman. For both of us that sudden confrontation in the alley between our houses had been at the same time embarrassing and frightening. The incident, curiously, started a subtle bond between us—something close, that only lovers or best friends can feel. Literally and metaphorically, our lives had intersected. Whenever I saw him I regarded him with respect, and though he didn't smile, his face was changed.

A month or two later I got up enough nerve to take my father to his house to look over a skinny-wheel bike he had for sale at an outrageous price of ten dollars. I felt strange standing there several feet away from the man I had once tormented with rocks and gestures. He seemed congenial, decent, like the other men in the neighborhood, except that he was deaf and dumb and could only grunt. My father and he couldn't agree on a price—which they kept handing back and forth on slips of paper—but by the time we parted and the junkman's eye caught mine, I realized we were no longer enemies.

PIGEONS

The two of us, at 14, stood there between the railroad tracks looking straight up at a piece of sun clearing the white east wall of the Nutrena Soybean mill. The mild shade was growing higher and higher up the wall, and just as the sun squeezed over, the noon whistle blasted.

We had plenty of time, and a good plan, and the men would be on the other side of the building eating lunch on the cool grass under the box elder trees.

Geesman was the lookout. I was the athlete, the climber. I patted my back pocket to make sure the pillow case was there. I was ready. From a pile of boards and railroad ties close to the wall, we grabbed a tie, each on one end, and slanted it against the building at a sharp angle, aiming for a window. I backed up several steps, then sprang forward onto the tie just fast enough to get my hands on the sill—held myself there a few seconds—then pulled up into the wide casing of the open window. I dropped down into the empty room, turned and stuck my head and arms out the window, and looked down. Already Geesman was holding up a long two-by-four from the wood pile. I took hold of the board, brought it through my hands, and slanted it crosswise in the window. I stood up on the sill and kicked some dried putty and splinters of glass off, for a place to stand in. I shinnied up the board high enough to get my hands on the sill directly above me. Then I pulled up into the second-story window, and dropped inside. My eyes weren't ready for the thick dark; I could see as far as two empty crates in the middle of the room. I turned around and looked over the edge at Geesman. He was waving up at me that everything was okay. I scraped some glass off the sill with my hand, and stood up in the clean spot. This time I didn't need a board—the steel rain trough was only a few feet above the window. I stretched until I got a firm grip on it, then jerked several times, testing its strength. I kicked my right foot up into the trough, hooked it with my gym shoe heel, and muscled up onto the roof, rolling over on my back on the warm, black asphalt.

For the first time, lying there, I heard the pigeons: a low dull cooing above me. I looked up in the direction of the sound. About 15 feet above me were two transformers on power poles side by side with some thick wires starting out of them. The lines were protected by a thin overhang held up by rafters, just above the top of the transformers. Between the overhang and the power lines, inside the rafters, were dark spaces. I knew the pigeons were in there. My climbing hadn't bothered them yet. They were still cooing and not flying around. I stood up quietly, and took one more look down at Geesman, who seemed no bigger than a doll, waving up. For a second I was light-headed.

The next climb had to be the quietest. I had to get on top of the overhang, then crawl far enough across it to be directly over the pigeons. I got up on an air vent, bear-hugged a transformer pole, and began to shinny up, slowly, carefully, to avoid splinters and to keep the birds cooing. When my head was just below the transformer, I shifted my weight onto a four-by-four a couple of feet from the pole, and kept climbing until I got hold of the overhang. I let my feet go, swung out free—hanging there a few counts—then pulled up on the top, rolling over several times to get clear of the edge.

Now, on my back again, I was above the birds, but still about 15 feet away. They'd heard the noise and had quit cooing. Four or five of them flew out over me, their white wings beating into the blue air. I lay quiet for a long minute. I listened to my pounding heart. Three birds came back, circled, landed on the lip of the overhang, and dropped down one by one between the wires, back to their shadowed nests. Apparently they hadn't seen me. I saw exactly where they went in. I waited another minute or so until I heard the steady low sounds, and then started crawling.

I stopped above the spot I knew they were under. I took the pillow case out of my back pocket and laid it beside me. I snaked forward silently, extending my head and chest over the edge. The overhang was unsturdy.

For some reason, I decided to test the wire that was close to the hole I would feel into. A wrist-thick wire wrapped with black tape. I reached down and touched it with my finger—*then I was dying—hung up by both hands on the wire—my neck screaming, bulging up close to explosion— currents of hot volts shooting up my legs, chest, arms—I was dying inside this electric second—seeing, feeling myself dying inside and outside my body—hung up by both hands—*

but then I dropped onto the roof, hard. Then my feet were more alive and lighter than ever, moving over the asphalt aiming for the place I had come out of on the roof before. Geesman must have seen my amazing vault over the rain trough, saw me getting bigger and bigger, the controlled fall, the swing into the upper window — legs, elbows, hands working in unison — the swing into the lower window, the sure-footed landing on the propped-up railroad tie, the leap to the solid ground — all this in a single, charged, unbroken motion. I whirled, crazy-eyed, and there was Geesman, back-stepping, speechless. All I said — three words — shot from my mouth like hot volts: *I got shocked.* My jaw collapsed on *shocked.* That word came out of my neck. Geesman kept watching me, waiting for more words.

We started across the tracks for home, my steps still electric, avoiding the rails with ease, Geesman still watching my eyes. We climbed the steep one-block street and Geesman kept on going while I turned north on Wall Street, climbing the steeper hill that led all the way to the top of the bluff and my brick house. When I got there I walked around back and into the yard heading straight for the pigeon coop near the garage. I tripped the latch, opened the little door, reached in and lifted out a pigeon. I held it as high as I could and let it explode out of my hand. I reached into the coop again and again. One by one I lifted all of them out, held them high and let go, their white wings beating, beating into the steep blue air over Wall Street.

Fist Heaven

"I was angry with my friend:
I told my wrath, my wrath did end.
i was angry with my foe:
I told it not, my wrath did grow."
—William Blake

A recurring fantasy of mine might make a good novella. It would go like this. A middle-aged man decides to locate the guys who intimidated or beat him up in his youth, and challenge them to a fight. One night he buys some beer, sits down at his phone and calls the men, some of whom are still living in his hometown, some elsewhere. When the listener balks or tries to laugh it off, the challenger gets belligerent and insistent. Finally, in all cases the challenge is accepted and a time and place—on the challenged's home ground—is set up. Then each chapter describes a fight and the story ends, say, when the last punch is thrown in the last flurry of fists.

My plot might even make a good movie—better yet, a documentary. In fact, (a ripple on the fantasy) if I could borrow some money and talk my deans into a sabbatical, I wouldn't just write it, I'd *do* it. Look the studs up, call them and, with director and video camera, begin to get it on in living color.

But I confess to a sense of fatalism in this matter of trying to even it up with my boyhood detractors. I might be in better shape than most of them, might surprise myself with the outcome of one or two fights, but my batting average wouldn't be respectable, probably. People don't change much. It's curious, for instance, how easily my two brothers and I, when we haven't seen each other for several years, quickly resume that old sibling chain of command whenever we get together. I'll always be in the middle, Bob will always be "little

41

brother'' (though he's bigger than Jerry and as big as I am), and Jerry, dominant voice and all, will always be the boss. Biology and culture combine powerfully here. The combination is apparently unbudgeable.

Recently in a small South Dakota town I unexpectedly met a man I hadn't seen for about 20 years, a school buddy of mine until we both moved away and went to different high schools in the mid 50s. He invited me to his house for dinner, and set a photo album before me with a couple of our school class pictures, from the third and fourth grades. What got our attention was not so much the two of us, but Manfred Graves, one of the toughest kids in Irving school. In the third grade shot he's sitting in front with his legs crossed Indian-style, with a healthy, assertive smile: the look of a young dominant male. (Who wouldn't be dominant with a name like Manfred?) I'm in the back of the group, looking slightly distracted. I remembered, studying the picture, that it was taken only a few months after I had moved into that Irving School neighborhood, a fact that may help explain my expression. After all, I was in strange territory.

But another reason for my look may be the fact that shortly after I started going to Irving, Manfred and I fought after school in an alley (I think I started it) and he manuevered me into a scissor hold on my stomach and squeezed the breath out of me. I struggled to say ''I give'' but nothing came out, not even air. I never bothered him again, though we did become friends. Early on, I learned the importance of making friends with the studs.

It seems that I was always second toughest in my class, as I was with my brothers. But everybody could take somebody. Manfred Graves could take me, who could take Franklin Thoms who could take John Griener who could take Eugene Paterson who could take Jim Hoover, and so on. One qualification. In the back row of that third-grade picture is a masculine-looking girl a head taller than everybody else except Roger Aikens, standing next to her. She could take everybody. Once several of us ganged up on her at recess and she singled me out with fierce fingernails that tore my shirt and raked my back. But because she was a girl she didn't count in the fighting scheme.

Not that we couldn't better our ranking by challenging and beating up the top dog or a kid above us. This was always possible and rumored, and sometimes we did shift positions in the hierarchy. In grade school it was a matter of someone having a grievance and saying to the one who wronged him: "I can take *you*."

"Oh yeah?" or "Huh!" the other would say, and then:

"Oh yeah?"

"Yeah."

"Huh!"

"Huh!"

This might go on for eight or ten more exchanges, and then peter out. Or one boy might recommend the after-school-in-the-alley-or-playground-get-together:

"Wanna make something out of it?"

If the challenged didn't want to make something out of it, he'd say "Huh" or "try to make me," or he would just walk away.

The after-school scenario often took only one or two swings and it was over; or, if it was obvious who would win when they faced each other, the weak would back down. It might also be a standoff, a fight that couldn't end because both boys were equal, in which case they would eventually quit, more or less together, huff it off and leave with their friends. You could always, of course, not show up. But that meant that you were a "chicken" or "chicken shit." Also, you risked being picked on by your challenger, and nobody wanted that.

Our fighting hierarchy was not based solely on brute toughness. It was more subtle than that. Bluffing was at the heart of it. All things equal, the ability to bluff was correlated positively with one's position in the pecking order. Those very few boys at the top could do it best; they could, for instance, stare you down. Ronnie Schwinck was a good starer, but his stare was different. Once on the playground we stood facing each other, our fists up, John L. Sullivan-style. He wasn't looking at me straight, but down at the asphalt, and yet I knew he saw me. I was hypnotized by the unbelievably white edge of his stare. It was the look of two male dogs when they meet and do their cocked, growling circles around each other. We stood there, ready, and neither of us took a swing.

Winning a fight was sometimes a matter of who got the first

punch in. One night when I was in junior high school, my brother Jerry and I and several others were standing on the shoulder of the highway outside the high mesh fence that enclosed the Riverside Amusement Park, watching the roller coaster rides. Ed Hanson and four or five of his Riverside gang came walking up the irrigation ditch alongside the highway. Hanson had a cocky cigarette on his lower lip. He and his gang stopped when they got between our gang and the fence, and Hanson said something insulting to us (I didn't hear the words but I caught the tone). Jerry, five years older than those in our gang and about Hanson's age, said: "Why don't you come up here and say that?"

Hanson climbed the bank toward us, alone, as the roller coaster cars were clicking to the top of the climb. Just as he got to Jerry (who was shorter and lighter) and seemed about to repeat himself, Jerry suddenly hit him so hard in the face that the cigarette shot up across the ditch and over the fence and Hanson fell and slid back down the bank, as the girls in the cars screamed above our heads and down into the trees and away. Hanson got up and hurried off with his buddies. That cigarette is still there in the grass under the roller coaster, glowing, tip-up, in my memory.

It wasn't my habit to run from a fight—I was aggressive (if a little shy) and liked to scrap—but I did now and then turn down an invitation to get smacked by someone obviously tougher than I was. Tom Blair, from another part of town, who later became a good friend, once socked me in the eye in the dark lobby of the old Iowa Theatre. I forgot who started it, but that was all it took to finish it. I staggered out the double doors crying, and the sun socked me in the eye again. Four or five years later, shortly after I had moved across town to the Leeds neighborhood—Blair's domain—he confronted me once more, after school.

"Hey Evans," he said, walking up to me from the other side of the street, "I hear you been telling people you whipped my ass." ("Whipped my ass" was more sophisticated than the phrases I was used to hearing). Tom had remembered when a friend of mine and I had beaten up on him shortly after the Iowa Theatre incident. Recalling the black eye, I wanted no part of this. I backed down. And that was enough to establish my place in the new neighborhood. I wouldn't be top dog in Leeds, either.

Almost all of our boyhood fights were fist fights, "fist heaven" as Tom Blair called them, laughing with brawling joy. We didn't use rocks or boards or our feet. To do so was to fight dirty. Our fights were wholesome. We simply squared off and slugged away until one of us quit or, as in the Graves fight, one got the other down and squeezed his neck or guts so hard he gave up. The only person who broke the rules with me was Max Lear, who once kicked me just under the ass. That fight didn't last long either, because of the long-legged strength of the kick and a brand-new engineering boot at the end of it.

I considered Lear's kick downright non-human. We could justify ganging up on someone — say, two guys on one, if the fight was fairly balanced — but to kick a person or throw something at him was outrageous behavior. Smacking a guy with both hands clasped together was also dirty. That's what Jim Graves, Manfred's older brother, did to a little karate expert at the Soos ballpark one night. The karate guy simply shook it off, waded into Graves with hydraulic fists and pounded him senseless. (Graves' response to that humiliation was delayed. About ten years later he took up karate, advanced several degrees beyond a black belt, and opened up one of the first martial arts studios in Sioux City.)

By the time we got to junior high school our notions about fighting began to blend with our notions about sports and athletes. Most of the boys in my crowd were athletes, like me, and we made a sharp distinction between ourselves and non-athletes. In the 50s in Sioux City, those of us who "played ball" practiced and performed earnestly and within the rules. We didn't drink or smoke or hang around much with girls (at least non-virgins), or keep late hours. And we generally disdained the greasers.

These boys wore tight tee-shirts, often with a carton of cigarettes tucked in a sleeve, jeans — low enough to expose the ass — and engineering boots. Instead of getting crewcuts or butches like us, they let their hair grow and slicked it back with hair oil or wax into a duck tail (we called it a duck ass in contempt). They drank beer and took out non-virgins, and most of them had one obsession: tinkering with cars in backyards and garages. They must have had dreams of chrome and pinging. At night and on weekends, in black leather jackets, they roared through the streets in suped-up V-8s with huge, shiny hubcaps and dual exhaust pipes that flashed and crackled as they passed, their left arm propped in the window like a stiff black flag.

The difference between greasers (and other non-athletes) and athletes was a pet theme of our junior high coach, Coach Speer. I recall one morning before classes when Speer and several of us were sitting on the cement steps of the school waiting for the bell.

"You take an athlete. . .," Speer said. He pointed to a line of elms across the street just outside the playground fence.

"Let's say you're in a war, and there's a hill over there. You ask the athlete to climb that hill and by God that athlete'll do it. The guy that's not an athlete will ask too many questions." (Speer should have known, we figured—he'd been in Korea, a Master Sergeant.)

Speer also made a distinction between "tough" and "rough." Tough meant the way you played football, for instance. Play hard, smack hard, bust your butt. Win, at all costs. Rough, on the other hand, meant the way you handled yourself in a fight if you had to fight. If you were rough you could take and take and take abuse but you could give back more than you took. There were still rules. You never picked a fight, and once in it you squared off with your opponent and fought fair. You never kicked him, you never hit him when he wasn't looking, you used only your hands (or legs if you were on the ground).

Some boys, like those in my crowd, were mainly tough; some were rough; some were neither. Then there was Bill Beston, who was rough *and* tough, the ultimate accolade.

Beston was a year older than most of us eighth graders, and bigger. He'd been held back in grade school because of his hearing. He had a hearing aid with a battery that was exactly the size of his shirt pocket where he kept it. He was our best lineman in football, a powerful left guard with muscles like hardballs. He couldn't hear the quarterback's signals so he had to turn his head and catch the snap of the ball under the center's legs.

46

When he talked, which was seldom, he was hard to understand. When he said the word "spiral" it sounded like "spirit," and he had gaps in his sentences where words should have been. His voice had a whiny twang in it.

Beston was quiet and kept to himself mostly, and he could read lips. If you were his friend, as we were, he tuned you in. If he didn't like you he'd turn the little wheel on his hearing aid battery to *off*. Nobody anywhere, as far as we knew, ever messed with him. He was the kind you have to almost kill before he gives up. He wouldn't pick a fight but he certainly wouldn't turn one down.

Beston's fights were famous at Woodrow. Once I saw him wade into a bullwhip held by the leader of the East Junior High gang, a guy about six-four. Bill wrapped the whip around his neck and threatened to kill him. It took several guys to pull him off.

Because we all assumed that Beston was the roughest kid in Woodrow Wilson Junior High, we curried his good will. We relied on him to back us up if we were threatened by somebody rougher than we were. Not that we actually sicced him on anybody; rather, he was our trump, our bluff. And he didn't seem to mind his role.

Ours was a popular clique; we got along with teachers, coaches, and the principal; we were out for sports and so we were considered dependable. A little arrogant and pushy, we scrapped now and then, but nobody got hurt. Our scheme of fair play/fair fighting worked, at least right up to the next to the last day of classes of our second year at Woodrow. Evidently Gene Pulcher didn't go for our scheme, much less for Bill Beston.

On one of those last days Lynn Peterson, Jerry Norton, and I were standing in the crowd at the finish line in the street outside the school, watching the finals of the eighth-grade intramural fifty-yard dash. (Because we were on the school track team, we couldn't compete in intramural events.)

First there was a puff of smoke, then the pistol shot, then somebody hollered *Here comes Pulscher!* Busting out of the blocks he was the only one standing straight up instead of leaning into his start to knife the wind, so right away he was in last place, running up on his toes, a little sideways, tall, piston-hipped, elbows and hands high and jerky, head level and steady as a cheetah's — not running so much as skittering on the asphalt like a loon across a lake. About half way he caught the pack and just powered through it, still picking up speed, still skittering, growing bigger and bigger, and he was at least five yards ahead of second-place Tobin when he broke the string and let up, coasting. When he stopped and turned around and walked back to the finish line, he had his hands on his hips and that trademark scowl on his face.

That's how Gene Pulscher won the eighth-grade intramural fifty. That's how he'd won the seventh-grade fifty, and that's how, a year later, he'd win the ninth-grade fifty. Skittering through the string with a scowl on his face.

We didn't like Gene Pulscher. He seemed to hide out behind his thick, black eyebrows all year, and then suddenly show up for the intramural fifty. Basically a greaser, he didn't go out for organized sports, and so we resented his success which had nothing to do with sweaty practice sessions, calesthenics that brought leg cramps, wind sprints that vacuumed the breath out of you.

Pulscher was the kind we couldn't tolerate: mysterious, aloof, independent, uninvolved, surly-looking, bigger than most of us. Not that we had any specific reason to dislike him — nor did we ever openly taunt him, or he us. But I always sensed something violent in him, something about to explode. So when he finally did explode one day at the end of the semester, I was shocked, like everybody else, and yet I had known that it was only a matter of time.

This is what happened.

It was in the afternoon of the day before the last day of school, and right after the last eighth-grade gym class. We were sitting around on benches after a shower, relaxed, drying ourselves and dressing and talking. Suddenly there was Pulscher (who wasn't in our gym class) coming fast through the doorway in that skittering sideways style of his, heading straight for Beston who was sitting on a bench by himself with his hearing aid and battery beside him on a towel. Beston was looking away, didn't see him, and Pulscher went up to him and let him have it with a terrific blow to the blind side of his face and he crumpled up and rolled backwards off the bench onto the wet towels on the floor. He was coiled up and holding his face with both hands. Then he looked up at Pulscher and he started to whimper. It was a weak, whiny cry from deep inside. Pulscher aimed his fist down at him: "*You* sonofabitch!" he said. He held that big square fist up for at least 10 seconds — waiting for Beston to get up — and then he whirled around and walked out of the locker room. We had to help Beston get his clothes on. When we left him a little later he was still holding his swollen face and whimpering.

That night after supper we had the perfect set-up in Peterson's basement. We took a burnt cork and charcoaled a huge face with thick eyebrows on the back of a cardboard box and nailed it to a door.

Peterson was first; it was his house. He smashed his fist through the mouth. Then it was my turn, and I got the left eyebrow. Then Norton's turn, then Peterson again, and so on. "Pulscher! Pulscher! Pulscher!" we kept saying.

Why did Pulscher do it? I remember exactly how I felt, then, about that act of violence. My feelings haven't changed in 30 years. I believe it was fear and envy that powered Pulscher's fist. He must have had a general grudge against us. We were arrogant and thought we had it made. He must have hated especially the idea that there was someone at Woodrow — Bill Beston — who could dominate him. He might have attacked all of us. If he could have slammed his fist into our collective face, I think he would have done it. That being impossible, he singled out the roughest. And his scheme worked. He changed everything with one smack of his fist. There would never be any retaliation.

Pulscher reminds me of those men in prisons serving life sentences. They have nothing to lose, so they might shove a knife in your back if you look at them wrong. Their habit, to quote Ted Hughes in a poem about hawks, is "tearing off heads." They are a paradox. It is fear that sets them off, and yet their whole life is a sustained, fearless effort to protect their concept of who they are. They will not ever be put off.

These men both fascinate me and scare me. There is something unspeakably terrifying and desperate about them. To respond to their violence is to invite more violence. Chairs

49

in the air, bullets, bombs. Lacking a sense of give and take in their relationships with other men, they are one-dimensional, single-purposed, like those survival machines, the sharks. They cruise through the world with a scowl, looking for disaster.

Girls

The first time I fell in love I was in the third grade. I loved Connie and Bonnie, identical twins who were at least a half a foot taller than I and two grades ahead. I didn't elevate one over the other but loved them both, totally. I doubt if they ever gave me a second glance though they might have known me as Little Evans because I had a brother about their age. They dressed exactly alike, with two pigtails each, and were inseparable.

One night at home when my sister was gone I raided the blue vase on her bedroom dresser. She didn't know that I knew where she kept her fanciest rings and necklaces. I took a ruby ring. One gift for my double love was enough. The next morning on the playground before the bell I approached to within about 30 feet of the twins without their noticing me. They were standing near the fence watching some other girls skipping rope. It was fall; the playground was matted with leaves — yellow, red, and brown, glistening in new light. I took the ring out of my pocket, threw it toward the twins and ran away. About half way across the playground I stopped and looked back. Nothing had changed. The twins were still standing there watching the kids skipping rope.

I decided there was no use going back for the ring after school — it was buried in leaves. But I imagined somebody finding it and wondering where it came from. Would they find out it was my sister's? Would they take it to her? Would she know who took it? Love gets complicated.

The playground incident was typical of my early infatuations. I was shy and frantic around the girls I was attracted to, and they were usually a grade or two ahead, cooler, and upwardly mobile.

51

Dixie, tall with sexy eyes, was another. I was in the seventh grade this time and she was in the eighth. One night after a party we were walking home together, mainly because we lived in the same neighborhood. When we got to the First Baptist Church where she was about to turn east and I north, she stopped, pinned me with her eyes and said:

"Sometime let's go to heaven together, Dave." (Whether or not she intended the religious irony, it took me 30 years to catch on.) I hadn't been to heaven with a girl but I knew right then that Dixie had been to heaven with a boy. (I'd already suspected it.) I also knew by the words and tone that she felt I wasn't quite ready for the trip. Nothing came to me to say and an awkward silence slipped in between us on the sidewalk. Then she gave me a high school kiss on the mouth and left.

The first girl I ever touched with lust in my heart was Barbara Townsend, who lived four houses down the street from me. It was a summer night; locusts were screaming in the black trees. I don't remember how we found ourselves together in her yard but I put my hand between her legs (she was wearing a white cotton dress). For a couple of seconds I felt a strange flatness, then took off running with my hand up the sidewalk home. I stopped by a tree in our yard. Secretly, guiltily, breathing hard, I braced myself with both hands against the tree to let the blood subside.

The first girl I "did it" with was the cousin of a friend who lived next door. I was in the eighth grade and Matty was a year or so younger, though (I was told) experienced with boys. It was the day before I'd be going to a weekend cub scout camp. The perfect set up: Matty was only a visitor and I was going away. By the time I got back nobody would remember. She was willing when I said we maybe ought to go up to the weeds, meaning the vacant lot behind our house. She pulled down her pants, I unzipped my jeans, put it in and that was it. Strictly mechanical; I don't recall what it felt like.

The guilt was building until a few weeks later when my mother confronted my younger brother about some transgression he'd committed with a girl (not as serious as what I'd done). After my brother, crying, confessed, I tossed in my transgression as an afterthought:

"Yeh, I did it too, but I won't do it again." I realized I was hedging on the sin by not being specific, but it didn't matter. What did matter was that I'd confessed outright. My mother was in her usual accepting mood whenever we boys owned up to something. I felt new.

It was always the other guy who got the girls. My younger brother, for instance. He told me once that a girl living up the street—who I assumed wasn't the kind—was constantly badgering him to feel her up (the current expression). So, I wondered, why didn't she ever badger *me*? My brother was getting tired of her and I could have moved in with her after one wink.

There was also the man at the summer carnival in South Sioux City—the one who introduced the strippers on the tent stage. He wore a cocked hat like a used-car salesman's, had a cane in one hand and a microphone in the other, and kept blaring to the crowd the names and measurements of a line of six or seven lovely young women in high heels and gowns, standing behind him. How I envied him! How nonchalant he was! Why wasn't he spending every second of his life, in a bed behind the curtain, say, with these women, one after the other?

Between the vacant lot experience and my sophomore year in high school when I started "going steady," my life with girls was pretty much a waiting game with me doing the waiting.

I had learned that girls didn't like boys who were too forward, but also that it was useless to expect them to come to you. Not that I didn't go after them sometimes. To us boys in that Wall Street junior high neighborhood, the girls were always "out there" if we could only find them. Some nights just after dusk a bunch of us would gather at a little store a block down the alley from my house. That was our meeting place, the starting point for our would-be exploits. I remember how assertive and exuberant and tough I felt when I shouted out with the others in my gang-voice:

"Let's get some ASS!" and then swaggered off up the middle of the street. And yet, just as I was shouting I knew, inside, that nothing was going to happen *that* night, no matter how much we wanted it to. Early on, I learned that there was a gap between desire and fulfillment.

These chest-pounding, yelling escapades were mostly ritualistic and harmless. The girls must have heard us a mile off; they were never there. But the really ugly gangs were those that formed spontaneously when girls *were* around. Only once, and regretfully, was I part of one of these gangs.

About a half a dozen of us junior high boys were sunning ourselves one afternoon on the banked cement that circled the Lief Erickson swimming pool. There was a girl we didn't know standing in waist-deep water, laughing, as if to herself. Then I noticed that a boy was diving underwater about 20 feet from her and she was backing up, trying to get away. He kept it up. Then two boys from our group got up and dove in and pursued the girl. She was backing up toward the fence that separated the shallow from the deep water. Now up to her shoulders, she was pushing the invisible hands away and still laughing.

Suddenly all of us were running and diving in. I was in front. I approached: saw the girl's bright blue suit, her pink legs, her feet bouncing on the bottom, her arms and hands thrashing among other hands—all this magnified inside a muffled violence. I pulled closer, pushed through others' hands, saw with wide eyes the delicate, bleached hair on her legs. I reached out, she bounced away. Nearly out of breath I lunged at her and felt between her legs, turned in another direction, separated myself from the mass of grabbing hands, emerged, sucked air, dove again, heading for deep water, kicked and pulled away as far as I could get without breathing.

Granny

The winter when I was 12 I did a pencil sketch of my maternal grandmother. I wish I still had that sketch; it would help me recall her. I had made the high cheekbone and newly-brushed, long, gray hair prominent. With the flat side of my pencil I had given the hair a dull sheen that would have rubbed off easily on clothes or hands if touched. The face, without glasses, was turned away and barely visible. No raven eye was there.

My sketch was intensely private. I had caught Granny— which is what everybody called her—in a vulnerable moment: with her hair down and glasses off and false teeth out. She hated those deep red dents on either side of her nose, and also she had to squint to see.

I had done the drawing at home and I didn't show it to Granny. I did show it to my mother, who praised its likeness. That surprised me since there was only a hint of face showing: the cheekbone. The picture was almost all hair.

Granny lived alone in a one-room upstairs apartment on Iowa Street, three blocks from our house. Just north of her apartment was a vacant lot owned by a strict and shy Jewish bachelor who used to pay me a nickel on Saturday mornings to turn his lights on because his religion forbade it. The lot had a sharp hill not quite long enough for sledding but just right for ''skiing'' down in leather boots or shoes, especially if the soles were waxed with a candle. If you lost your balance going down and forgot to grab your head with both hands you could crack it on the ice, hard as marble. (It sounded like two bowling balls colliding.) The headache might last all day. Sometimes four or five of us made a chain by holding onto the waist of the kid in front of us and went down together. That way when one fell all fell and it wasn't as hazardous, though you might get kicked in the head or face by a flying boot.

But that winter I wasn't supposed to be doing any sledding or skiing. I had had some pains in my chest the summer before, often after pole vaulting or swimming. Though the pains weren't frequent I still had them; I couldn't inhale all the way to the end of a breath without feeling a knife in my heart. My parents became concerned when I began to wake them up in the middle of the night. When Granny recommended a Dr. Dobson on the West Side, my mother took me to see him. A fat, jolly black man with a face that resembled a lump of brown dough with pock marks in it, he knuckled lightly on my chest while listening to my heart with his cold stethescope.

"Pooty good little ticka," he said, "but you gotta slow down, David. You gotta slow down awhile."

He gave me a note to take to my principal. It said no sports or gym classes for the "balance of the school year," which meant for the next five months. He told my parents I'd have to get plenty of rest and plenty to eat so I could outgrow my sickness, rheumatic fever.

"Now you listen to Old Doc Dobson, he'll fix you up," Granny said when I told her the news. I had always been her favorite, constantly running errands for her: taking out the garbage, going to the drug store and the Atlas Market. She had come to depend on my being there at least a couple of times a week (her apartment was on the way to school) and certainly on weekends. She always had cookies and candy around, and often cold pork chops to heat up or eat cold. She was insulted if you didn't help yourself, and that went for my friends as well.

When I was a young boy on the acreage she had given me the name of Snakehips because she thought I was too thin. Whenever I came through her door she'd say something like:

"Well, what do you know, if it ain't ole Snakehips himself."

Now, after my diagnosis, Granny could be even more indulgent. I was impressionable and she had a strong influence on me. She knew me well. It was as if, around her I was made of glass and she could see right into my thoughts with her dark eyes. She also had more time than my parents to indulge in sympathy. The chest pains scared me; I couldn't handle pain. She convinced me that her place was the place to be: she'd keep me quiet and fatten me up, exactly what Dr. Dobson had prescribed.

Granny's apartment became a second home to me that winter. Our relationship wasn't the usual one between grandparent and grandchild but more like a symbiosis. Each benefitted from the other's presence: she had me to run errands and to talk to and play cards with; I had a good listener too and a warm, quiet room to relax in as well as all the food and goodies I wanted. We were partners in sympathy.

No doubt she needed more sympathy than I did. Well into her 70s she was always battling colds and other maladies. Some days she simply stayed in bed because she was too weak to get up. And she had never been popular with my parents and other relatives. Generally they avoided her and labelled her as devious: one who wouldn't hesitate to start up an ugly rumor about somebody just to cause trouble. "Flannel mouth" and "pure poison" were two epithets I was used to hearing at home. I might have nodded assent when I heard these words about Granny, but they meant nothing. To me she was good.

I remember more about Granny's room than any other room of my childhood. The iron bed, with one army blanket for a bedspread and another for a spare folded squarely at the foot, was next to a double, wrap-around bay window with a good view of Iowa Street. I usually sat on the bed instead of a chair. I took naps or, propped up by two pillows and with a drawing pad on my knees, drew strange designs, in ink or pencil, which Granny called "modern art." Or I looked out the window and watched the kids sledding down the Street or skiing down the vacant lot hill.

About two feet above the bed were two drooping strings tied to the head bedpost. Each string was connected to a gold chain hanging from the apartment's two ceiling lights, one in the middle of the room and one in the kitchen. These strings allowed Granny to turn the lights on or off without having to get out of bed.

On the other side of the bed was a small, wooden night stand (which I still have) with a lamp and an alarm clock. Also on the stand were four inevitable items: a pack of Raleigh cigarettes, a jar of Vicks, a box of Smith Brothers Cherry

Cough Drops, and a box of Kleenex.

At the foot of the bed was a black, hump-back trunk whose musty contents I loved to examine. There was a small box of sulfur which, the first time I sniffed it, stuck in my nostrils and I thought I was actually dying; several balls of string (Granny collected it); a brown stole consisting of two flattened mink or muskrat heads sewn, staringly, nose to nose; a cigar box containing old coins, mostly Indian Head pennies, some flint arrow heads, and an intricate-looking gold watch with a lid you could open or snap shut (I still have it). The rest was mostly things that had belonged to Granny's only siblings, two brothers who had died: some clothes, razors, a razor strop, two shaving mugs, two brushes, and several pairs of suspenders.

There were three chairs in the room, two flimsy cloth-backed ones and a rocker that Granny sat in when she wasn't bedridden—to read the paper, work a crossword puzzle, listen to the radio, wind her strings, or talk. Or just sit.

The kitchen consisted of a portable stove and refrigerator, cupboards, a table and four chairs. All of this was squeezed behind a dividing counter in an area about the size of a small pantry.

Sometimes, it seemed, hours passed in that room before a sound was heard. It could be as quiet as the little round world inside a glass snow globe. Or was it rather that, in this environment of drowsy clarity, all the sounds were silent sounds? The slow squeaking of the rocker as Granny read or wound her strings or filled in a crossword puzzle; the intermittent hissing of the radiator; the ticking of the clock which is the same ticking I still hear from any clock in any quiet room; the sound—if I listened closely—of breathing: my own breathing, Granny's breathing, filling the room; the *puff puff* of the Vicks vaporizer when Granny had a cold; the scuttling—most of all the scuttling!—of dilapidated, felt slippers across the floor; the sudden sniffling into a Kleenex.

We talked. Granny told me stories. If you traced her family back far enough, she said, you'd find out that on the Whitman side (her maiden name) she was related to the great poet. And then the one about Pike's Peak:

"When you go to Pike's Peak some day you look at the

graves at the foot of that mountain. Look for the name Whitman. My dad was the first man to be buried at the foot of Pike's Peak.'' There had been a gold claim, an argument, a fight. Granny's dad had been shot and buried there. It sounded famous to me.

Once she had died on an operating table and then after the doctor and nurses gave her up for dead, she woke up. She died of ''deadly pneumonia'' and God brought her back. Telling me this her eyes blurred with tears:

''I was walking with the angels, Dave.''

We played a card game called Cassino. She always knew what cards I had and usually won. I didn't enjoy cards and still don't, but I enjoyed playing with her just because she took the game so seriously. She made me laugh watching her darting black eyes, her spidery fingers.

When I went to the store for pork chops, our favorite dinner on weekends, she reminded me to go straight to the butcher :

''Now you tell him you want the best chops for Granny. He knows me. I'm one of his best customers.'' I had to be sure to get the Raleigh cigarettes with the coupons, which she pasted in books until she had enough to buy something with: a toaster, a kitchen knife, or a gift for me. She made sure I was paid for my errands. A quarter here, a dime there. But she would press money into my palm whether I earned it or not.

When it came to money she trusted nobody. She seemed to have more than enough of it, though she often complained about the government cutting her checks. She kept her bills rolled up tightly and wrapped with rubber bands and fastened with a safety pin to something under her housedress. Whenever she gave me money for groceries or drugs, she would say:

''Now you make sure you count your change.'' She usually knew exactly how much change I had coming.

All the extra food and all the quietness and comfort that winter had a positive effect on me. My report card said that I grew five inches and gained 30 pounds. Granny was quick to take credit for my outgrowing the rheumatic fever. The chest pains were gone. By summer I was back on the playgrounds and baseball diamonds. I still saw Granny often, still ran errands for her and spent time with her, but not nearly as

much as I had in the winter.

Something happened that summer that still perplexes me. One day I was in a neighborhood grocery store with some friends. On impulse, I bought a pack of Raleighs, saying it was for my grandmother, which was the truth. Later, alone, I went to her apartment and gave her the cigarettes.

"I don't want no cigarettes," she said sharply. Her voice was mean, a stranger's. I knew she wasn't that sick because she was up. Apparently she was angry because she hadn't sent me to the store for the cigarettes. She didn't make me take them back, but she made me regret that I'd bought them for her on my own.

*   *   *

After I got married and went away to college I of course saw less and less of Granny. Yet we continued to get along well. Whenever I was in Sioux City I went to see her. Even after I had quit football and had bulged up to over 200 pounds, she kept reminding me of my weight:

"Well, what do you know, ole skin and bones himself," she'd say when I visited her. I never was fat enough for Granny, she still had pork chops around to fatten me up and she still gave me money, which I was reluctant to take.

Her health began to deteriorate rapidly the first year I was in graduate school. Finally, when she couldn't take care of herself anymore, my parents, who were living in Tennessee, had her put in a nursing home. She hated it. Growing senile and decrepit, she lashed out at the aids and nurses, accusing them of neglect, of rotten food, of stealing her money. A relative of mine who worked at the nursing home described some nasty scenes, one involving an aid who suddenly quit in frustration because of Granny's abuse.

One day my sister called me in Iowa City and said Granny was in the hospital and dying, and that I should try to make it home. Granny was barely conscious but she was calling out for me, only me. My wife and I drove to Sioux City the next day. I went to the hospital; the nurse in charge said that Granny was going fast.

61

I went into her room alone. Her eyes were closed, she was mumbling, without teeth. I spoke to her and dabbed her forehead with a washcloth. I doubt if she understood who I was but now and then I heard my name on her dry lips. The nurse kept checking her vital signs and, pulling back the sheet, the color of her legs.

"They start to turn blue when they're dying," she said.

I stayed with her for several hours, then left for a sandwich and a beer with my wife and sister. When we got back to the hospital the nurse said Granny was very close to death. I went in alone again. Her breathing seemed tortured, as if each breath fell from the end of a knife blade of air. Maybe a half hour passed. Then, with my hand on her forehead, suddenly she took two hard deep breaths and let go.

The Story Of Lava

Every time I smell Lava soap it is 1948.
My father is bending over a long sink in the
pressroom of The Sioux City Journal *at 6 A.M.,*
his grey long-underwear peeled down over his
white belly, a thin bar of Lava tumbling over
and over slowly in his ink-stained hands.
The morning news has passed through his hands
out into the morning streets into the hands
of sleepy boys who fold it a certain way and
fling it on porches and steps, but that is not
my story. Lava is my story and the morning
news that Lava can't rub off. It is my father
bending over a sink, a thin bar of Lava tumbling
over and over and over slowly in his cloudy hands.

According to a family rumor, by the time he was 20 my
father had read every book in the Sioux City Public Library.
This was easy to believe as a boy, but not anymore. And yet,
knowing my father's ravenous reading habit, I don't doubt
that he *tried* to read every book in the library.

There is an anecdote out of his youth that I have on good
authority, my aunt. Around 18 and not long after he had
bought his first car, a rickety Model A, he was driving to work
one morning when the car stalled. He got out and instead of
lifting the hood and peering under it, or kicking the tires, he
climbed on the hood, stood up, and began to gesture wildly
and shout like an auctioneer at the drivers going around him
and the people on the sidewalk:
"Who'll gimme 10?. . . Who'll gimme 12?. . . ."

He sold the car on the spot, pocketed the money and walked the rest of the way to work, cheerfully.

My father was one of those earnest working class sons who came of age during the Depression. His father, a railroad man, died in a mental institution in his 30s. His mother, a pleasant woman with a sunny, puffy-cheeked countenance, was born in a seaport town in Norway, where she was known as an excellent ice skater as a girl. My father had to quit school in the eighth grade and take odd jobs to help his struggling family. One job, peddling *The Sioux City Journal* on downtown street corners, involved hanging around the *Journal* building. At 17 he jumped at the chance for a steady job: a pressman's apprenticeship. At 22 he got his journeyman card, and for the next 30 years, to support himself, my mother, and five children, he worked in the same dingy pressroom where he had gotten his start.

He also began to write around 17 or 18 — short stories, poems, essays — publishing a few things in various magazines, later reviewing books for the *Journal's* Sunday paper. (An editor of a high school literature anthology once "bought" a short story from him, but no money came.) What made his life difficult and desperate was the growing realization that he had missed his calling — that he was an intellectual and a writer and therefore he was wasting his talent if not his life by having to work mostly with his hands. The realization began to gnaw at his soul. With only a seventh grade education he knew he was trapped in the pressroom until he died, unless he educated himself, at home after work.

I have two main images of my father from my childhood. I see him sitting, nearly horizontal, on his tan, naugahyde recliner in the living room, reading, his big feet with nylon argyle socks looming over the edge of the chair's flip-up bottom. Or I hear him in the basement, pecking away with his two index fingers on his relic Woodstock typewriter.

The predominance of these two images means to me that he had little time for the usual responsibilities of fatherhood. Most fathers in our culture work an eight-hour day and then go home to the more important (as they see it) business of spending time with their families. They take for granted the separation of work from home life. It was not that way with my

64

father. He had two kinds of work: one was involuntary, the other voluntary. The first he did for a living, the second out of a need to better himself. He believed he was gifted and that the only way to respond to his gift was to cultivate it. His desire was to be a writer and to make a living as a writer.

We children didn't experience the daily give and take with our father that most children experience. Not that he didn't spend time with us and take us places. He did, but rarely. And yet maybe the infrequency of these moments of indulgence made them even more precious when they did occur. There were some bright moments with him and my two brothers.

When the Ringling Brothers-Barnum-and-Bailey Circus came to town in the summer, we would all get up before the sun and walk (we didn't have a car in those days) a couple of miles down to the circus grounds near the Floyd River. We watched the men unload the animals and gear from the train; saw the huge, silent, slow-motion elephants wading into the river to drink; saw the iron stakes disappearing into the wet grass under the rhythmic swing of sledge hammers, as the tents grew over our heads like inflating mountains.

About once a summer he took us fishing. This time we walked across the Wall Street viaduct, past the stockyards and Armour's and Swift's to Half Moon Lake, which lay below a bluff known as "Polock Hill" because of the many Polish families living on it. We fished for bullheads and crayfish, which we called "craw-dads." Our father didn't fish but helped us thread nightcrawlers on our hooks and showed us how to cast. When he wasn't looking we'd toss a crawdad onto the highway running alongside the lake and watch the creature back up and raise its little pinchers like duel swords when a car's shadow swept over it. If it wasn't lucky enough to escape to the side of the highway and slip back into the lake, a wheel smashed it flat into the concrete.

There were occasional family outings too. In later years when we had a car we packed it with all seven of us along with fried chicken and potato salad in crocks covered with towels and headed for Brown's Lake. We had a favorite secluded spot on the north side of the lake where we could swim undisturbed and where even Dad could go in without being embarrassed about the chronic rash on his elbows and knees. I often watched him. He was a big man, nearly six-two, with long legs and bulging calves. How strange it was to see him in a bathing suit, this man who spent so much of his time indoors reading and writing. His body was the color of bone dust. He never swam long, just waded in and dog paddled a few minutes, took a few strokes on his back or stomach, and walked back up on the beach. It was obvious that he had once been a powerful swimmer; he could easily have caught us boys if he'd wanted to, though we were good swimmers and spent much of our summers at the city pools and the rivers.

Even here at the lake, far from home on a beautiful summer day, he seemed preoccupied. His big white body was with us; his mind was at home.

Though we rarely could engage him in play, we could talk him into reading to us. Sometimes in winter when it was too cold to be outside—so cold and windy the windows hummed—we sat around his chair with bowls of popcorn and listened to stories. Ghost stories, or stories by Jack London, Oscar Wilde, the Brothers Grimm, Sherlock Holmes, Booth Tarkington, Ernest Thompson Seton, and others. I enjoyed most the animal stories by Seton. I was always asking to be read the one called ''Lobo, The King of the Carrumpaw.'' One scene stays with me. Lobo's mate Blanca is surrounded by

bounty hunters on horseback and lassoed around the neck by ropes. The men pull in several directions at once and Blanca, struggling at first, falls limp and dies in agony. The scene left me blinded by tears.

My father could be moody. Sometimes forced to work overtime because of an extra edition or because the press had broken down, he came home feeling edgy. On those days, or when his writing wasn't going well, the best place for us kids was outside.

One brief summer vacation turned briefer because of him. My mother had organized an overnight trip to Lake Okoboji, 100 miles away. We had packed a picnic, swimming suits, inner tubes and were on the way. Mother was driving, as usual, and Dad was next to her. I had noticed his quietness, which was building with the miles. Evidently the two had been quarreling. Then, just as we turned east on a county road and saw the sign saying "Okoboji 25 miles," suddenly he turned to her and said:

"I don't want to go, take me home."

Mother remonstrated but to no use. She must have realized the rangle that lay ahead—in a packed car so far from home—if she protested or, worse, ignored him and drove on. She slowed down at the nearest turnoff, made a U-turn and we headed back to Sioux City. It was a gloomy 75 miles for all of us.

There was another incident in the car, this time in town. I was about 10 and between the two of them when Mother, steering with a scowl from an argument, took a downhill Court Street S-curve so loose the tires were screaming, so Dad clenched his big square fist up on the dashboard and braced himself to say, shakily, out the windshield:

"If you don't slow this car down I'll do something you'll regret. . ."

Now it was her turn to talk so she increased the tires' screaming by tromping on the gas until the big fist—but not her scowl—unclenched itself and we fell a steep block and then levelled out but kept speeding right through the school zone. Mother had won, as usual.

*   *   *

Not a single book I inherited from my father has anything written in it except his name, "A.C. Evans," inside the front cover. Even though most of the books he bought—from the Salvation Army and Goodwill stores or garage sales—were used, he never underlined sentences or wrote in the margins. Books were for reading and re-reading; to write in them was a sacrilege.

He spoke of his favorite writers as if he knew them personally. One night when I was in high school and looking through his book shelves for something to report on for a class, he said to me:

"You know, Dave, some day if you don't have any more friends you can always have books."

The words were serious and close. At the time I thought I understood, but now, 25 years later, I'm not sure. Were books *that* important to him? Had he just given up on a friendship, or had a friend died? Or did he mean that the older you get the fewer friends you need, so that books take their place? Evidently I'm still too young to understand.

Whenever he came to a passage in a book that moved him or made him laugh he'd yell for my mother and read it to her if she was nearby. If she was in the kitchen he'd yell "Ruth!," spring off his chair and, with his eyes still fixed on the lines rush into the ktichen in his stocking feet and detain her from dishes or ironing, and read to her.

"My God," he'd say, "What about *that?*" and she would usually like it too. Then he'd rush back to his chair and read until he came to another gem worth quoting aloud.

His memory for such passages was remarkable, probably the best I've ever known. To watch him mumbling the words to himself, his eyes tightening under his horn-rimmed glasses, a smile spreading on his face, was to watch the machinery of memory itself working. He didn't *need* to mark these pages—once he read them well they were his, forever. And he loved to recite (he did some acting for the Sioux City Community Theatre). He could quote Shakespeare's famous soliloquies from the tragedies and histories, and not just single lines but large chunks from many writers: Anatole France, Marcel Proust, Andre Gide, Voltaire, H.L. Mencken, Sinclair Lewis, Robert Benchley, Clarence Day, Ernest Dowson,

Herbert Spencer, Thomas Huxley, G.B. Shaw, and Thomas Wolfe, his favorite American writer.

It didn't take much to get him going on a long quote if he was in the right mood or if he'd had a few beers. One of his favorite soliloquies was the opening of *Richard the Third*. He'd back up against a wall and coil up like a serpent and begin, sneeringly:

"Now is the winter of our discontent. . ."

Another soliloquy he liked even better began:

"Aye, Edward will use women honorably."

When he spoke this line he'd raise his eyebrows on "honorably." He loved to say that word.

We had an old phonograph and my father had bought a record of John Barrymore reading from Shakespeare's plays. Occasionally he went to his bedroom and got the record (made of slate) out of his top dresser drawer where he hid it from the sun and careless hands. If he couldn't get anyone to listen with him he'd play it for himself. I heard it enough times to remember the angry, knife-like voice of Barrymore's Hamlet:

Bloody, bawdy villain!
Remorseless, treacherous, lecherous, kindless villain!

My father had another passion: the voice of Enrico Caruso. Opera was a family tradition with him, since one of his aunts had been an opera singer in the East. I remember when he bought his first good phonograph, a Mahogany-colored, plastic portable. On weekends he might spend hours listening to Caruso. I sometimes heard him in the shower booming out or lulling those great songs from "Aida," "Vesti La Guibba," and "O Sole Mio."

*   *   *

The old *Journal* pressroom was under the sidewalk on the north side of the building. As a young boy I used to stand on that sidewalk with my mother, brothers, and sisters, looking down through the plate glass windows. I can still picture my father in his hand-made paper cap, looking up at us and waving. If the press was running, I felt the sidewalk vibrating

under my shoes and heard a muffled roaring through the dark, thick glass. Four or five pressmen were stationed around the floor. At either end of the press a huge roll of paper was whirling and, if you stared long enough, slowly shrinking. The rest was long sheets of paper, blurring rivers of words — shooting up, angling sharply on rollers, cascading, angling, shooting up, levelling out and then, at the folder where the foreman was standing, the morning papers were coming out bunched up, accordian-like. Thirty thousand, 40,000, 50,000 papers an hour. The louder the faster. Now and then the foreman reached down and plucked out a paper and opened it

70

and—unlike a man in slippers on Sunday morning!—inspected it for flaws, closed it up and inserted it back into the white accordian. Good news to him was clean, black ink and perfect margins.

When I was about 10 my father sometimes took me with him on Saturday mornings to pick up his check. I remember well the increments of sound if the press was running. (There was nothing louder than the pressroom when the press was revved up, nothing quieter when it was off.) First, we opened the door to the building and heard a high metallic humming. Next, the heavy, steel door to the pressroom, and the humming changed to a roaring blast. Then, down 20 or 30 greasy steps into the pressroom itself. The lower you stepped the more deafening the noise became, until, at the bottom the sound stung your ears. In this world, conversation was impossible. If you had to you could yell into somebody's ear, but that hurt even more. You could, like the pressmen, read lips and use facial expressions, body english and gestures. Or wait until the press stopped.

It was also a world of ink. Ink so thick on the floor it felt like forest loam under your feet. Ink in the air, sparkling like tiny black snowflakes against the florescent lights. Ink blackening your nostrils and nostril hair. Ink filling in the lines on your face, palms, and knuckles, ink caked under your fingernails. Ink in your coffee during a coffee break, ink in your sandwich at lunch. Nothing, not even gritty Lava soap, could get you completely clean. In a slack moment, sometimes the younger men—my father among them, I'm told—had a contest. They took turns leaping against the whitewashed wall of the lunchroom to see who could make the highest mark with inky fingertips.

The pressroom was a dangerous place to work. (This machinery was fast becoming obsolete and would be replaced in the 60s by quieter, safer, off-set machinery which involves photography.) The heavy, awkward, sharp-edged printing plates could cut hands or break a foot if dropped. Even more dangerous was the procedure of locking in and adjusting the plates on the press. When I was in my mid-teens and old enough to work, my father occasionally had me fill in for a sick flyboy, an all-purpose errand runner. One night I had the job of working the start and stop buttons as the pressmen locked in the plates for the next run. It wasn't difficult; all I had to do was push the red or green button when my father, night foreman, told me to. But with one precaution: I was supposed to yell out "UP" just before I pushed the start button so that the pressmen could take their hands off the press. I was tired, not used to staying up all night, and once I forgot to call out the warning. Luckily, nobody had a hand on a plate or he might have lost a finger. My father reprimanded me, mostly with a look. I never made that mistake again.

Many of the pressmen were missing a finger or two or were scarred from various accidents around the press. In 30 years of handling plates and working the dummy—a portable elevator that carried plates down from the second floor where they were cast—my father didn't have a single nick on his hands. Around machinery he was a man in earnest.

*   *   *

My father had once been an excellent athlete—bowler, softball pitcher, golfer, sprinter—but he had given up organized sports in his mid-20s. He was 30 when I was born so I never got to see him perform as an athlete in his prime. That is all the more regrettable since I have been sports crazy from the age of five or six when I first learned to smack a baseball on our acreage in the country.

I did get to see him bowl a few times when, in his 40s, he was reluctantly substituting on a neighborhood team. I could tell he had once been very good: his delivery was strong and smooth, the sizzling ball bit into the wood and hooked sharply into the pocket. But he was obviously rusty. That was 15 years after he had bowled on teams and in tournaments. He seemed impatient, probably thinking that the only way he could bowl well was with pure luck. Because he was such a worker and needed to improve anything he took up, he never enjoyed recreational sports for their own sake.

As an athlete myself, I was always curious about his athletic past. In those rare moments when he played catch with me in the yard, I noticed how careful he was to loosen up his arm before he put any steam on the ball or threw a curve. There was an easy grace in his movements, the grace of a natural ball player. Warmed up, his throws stung my hand even when he wasn't trying to throw hard.

One day when I was in the ninth grade a few friends and I were kicking a rubber ball around in our yard after school. Somebody kicked it high into one of the cottonwood trees that bordered our yard and our neighbor's. The ball stuck in a crotch about 30 feet up. We kept trying to knock it down with a softball, but nobody could hit it. The father of a friend next door was raking leaves. This man, a janitor at the grade school nearby, was always playing catch with his two boys and had himself been a fine athlete in his youth. He came over when he saw we weren't getting anywhere. Short and squat, with a cigar sticking out of his yellow teeth, he asked for the ball. He maneuvered under the tree, loosened up his arm like a pro pitcher, and let the ball go, missing his target by a few feet.

"Gimme that ball again," he said, and one of us retrieved it and he threw again, missing badly. Again we gave him the ball, he fired up into the branches and missed. His face was flushed from the effort, the cigar was nodding in his teeth from hard breathing.

"You'll have to wait for a stiff wind," he said, and went back to his raking.

My father had apparently heard the commotion and came up out of the basement. We pointed up into the branches at the problem.

"Let me see the ball," he said. He took it, stood under the tree, looked up, aimed, and let the ball go, underhanded but with force. The rubber ball flew out of the tree. How I responded to that! And yet there was no exuberance on his face—he looked like a man who had simply done a task. He turned and went back down to his typewriter.

Though he took an interest in the sports careers of my older brother, an accomplished pole vaulter, and me, my father was not as indulgent as most fathers of good athletes. But in the football season of my senior year, things changed. Not only would he readily throw a football around but he began to ask

73

me to play catch. He was working days then and on the way home from the *Journal* he would get off the bus near the high school to watch me practice. He never came through the gate to the scrimmage field itself but stood outside the high mesh fence. I suppose he thought that standing with the coaches and subs on the sidelines would embarrass me, since he was the only father who showed up. His visits became regular. I got used to glimpsing, out of the corner of my eye, that tall figure with a paper in his hand. I'm sure I ran harder and faster because he was there.

I was doing well that last season, and each game intensified his interest. At home games (my parents went to away games too) he left my mother in the bleachers with the other mothers, huddling together like sparrows in the crisp September night, and came down to the sidelines with all the proud fathers, to follow the action up and down the field. I couldn't acknowledge him directly, that being unheroic in those days, but I felt his presence under the tall eyes of stadium lights, and singled out his voice among the other manly voices.

My best habit was busting through the line on off-tackle plays and sprinting, untouched, my knees pumping like pistons, down the sidelines for 70- and 80-yard touchdowns. Somehow, as if he had run down the sidelines with me, my father was always there, near the end zone, when I turned around and started back to the extra-point huddle. He would say, "Nice run, Dave," and I would nod, modestly.

Homecoming was everything it had been glorified to be. Earlier that week I was shown on television running with the ball, called an "all-City candidate" by the sports announcer, and my coach praised me highly in the paper. When the announcement of Homecoming King came on Friday, the day of the game, I was disappointed by not making it, though I was chosen as an Attendant. Just before I left home for the game my father said he would buy me a new suit if I scored at least two touchdowns.

I scored three that night, but I don't remember the game well: my memory blurs with other games, the lights, the cheers, the band blaring, the school song, the rhythmic stomping of feet in the bleachers. After my longest run—a 39-yard run around right end—I suddenly felt sick in the end zone and vomited. (The night before I had been up late with my girlfriend, a cheerleader I would marry a month out of high school). I heard my father's concerned voice:

"You alright, Dave?"

I was fine, and went back to the huddle for the extra point, which I kicked with a shaky leg, the ball barely clearing the uprights.

I had scored most of my team's points; we had beaten a school from Orange City, a little Dutch town 30 miles north.

When I got home my father was joyous. Knowing I had been disappointed because I hadn't been chosen King, he said:

"You were the king tonight, Dave."

The next morning the *Journal* article about the game called me a "fleet halfback," a "slashing runner," and gave me most of the credit for the Homecoming win. (I'm sure I didn't think of it then — being so young and full of myself — but now, almost 30 years later, I can appreciate my father's pride whenever he was in the pressroom and my name was in the paper. I imagine him standing there, down in that roaring pit, in a cocked paper cap, looking up at those rivers of paper repeating my name 40,000 times an hour!)

That same morning my father took me downtown on the bus. As we walked through the door of a clothing store not far from the *Journal,* the owner, who obviously knew my father, greeted us and said:

"Who's that you got with you, Art, the halfback?"

"That's right," my father said, beaming.

I tried on a light beige suit, noticed how the coat expanded my shoulders in the mirror, and my father took out his billfold and paid the man 30 dollars. We said goodbye and left, my father carrying the box with my suit in it under his arm. Walking beside him down the street to the bus stop, I never felt closer to him and never saw him happier.

When the All-City selections were announced in the paper at season's end, I was on the second team — another disappointment. But since I went to one of the two small city high schools and the selection process tended to favor the three big schools, I could still be proud. My father brought home a handful of neatly scissored and trimmed copies of the

All-City list from the *Journal*. He knew my height and weight were listed wrong so he went to work with an ink pen. I still have the clippings, all 20 or so. On each one the 5'10'' reads 5'11'' and 170 pounds reads 174 pounds. He got it right, in case anybody wanted to know.

The following winter I began to get letters from colleges and small universities in the region. I'm sure my parents felt that the only way I would get a college education was on a football scholarship; they couldn't afford to send me or even help me much. Two more reasons made a scholarship important: my girlfriend and I were getting more and more serious with each other; and I was of an impractical bent, not the go-getter-industrious type (like my brother, for instance), so college was the best route to a suitable job.

During the basketball season, coaches from various colleges were in Sioux City recruiting players. Some of them showed up at the school and watched me working out on the basketball team and talked to the coach. Several came to my house and spoke with my parents and me. I remember one such visit. The

head football coach and an assistant from South Dakota State University had written my parents and set up a time to come see all of us. That night my father was pacing the floor; I was sitting on the sofa in my t-shirt. When I said I needed to change my shirt, he stopped me:

"Wait, Dave, why don't you leave your t-shirt on."

"Really?" I said. I didn't think I was properly dressed.

"That way they can see your build; they like to see a player's build, you know."

I left the t-shirt on, even though it made me feel a little self-conscious when the coaches came.

Between my spring graduation and the fall, my life changed drastically. I got married; my wife, with still a semester of high school to finish, gave birth to a baby boy several months premature, and he died hours later; I enrolled in a college 100 miles from home; and my parents, younger brother and younger sister moved to Pressman's Home, Tennessee, where my father became the editor of his union's magazine.

There is one memory of my father from that summer—my last at home—that is painful to recall yet terribly important to me. The morning after the night our baby died, I lingered in bed in my basement bedroom, trying to both forget and make sense out of what had happened. When I heard footsteps coming down the stairs I pulled a blanket over my head. It was my father. He sat down next to me on the bed and quietly asked me how I was doing. I kept my head buried, muttering that I was okay. There was a long moment of silence, an awkwardness. Then suddenly he broke down and began to sob. I looked over my blanket, I couldn't believe this: I'd never seen a grown man even cry, and here was my father sitting close to me on my bed and sobbing uncontrollably. All he could get out was:

"Everything will be alright, Dave. . . everything will be alright."

We cried together for a couple of minutes, then he patted me on the head and left. For several more minutes I saw him standing between some sheets hanging on the clotheslines. Then he went upstairs.

*   *   *

In September the *Journal* reported in an article about my father that he had "realized a lifelong ambition to become a professional writer" by taking a job as editor of his union's magazine. The article was only partly right: yes, at 47 he had finally realized a dream, but not his best dream. It must have gradually occurred to him over the years that a writing career would have to be connected with his job as a pressman. He had read widely in the history and politics of unionism and had contributed articles to his union's magazine. Given his pressroom experience, writing skills, knowledge and enthusiasm, he was certainly qualified for his new job. Even though he wouldn't be able to concentrate on essays and stories like the writers he admired and emulated, at least he had escaped the pressroom. But more than that—he had found a job for which his writing talent and work had prepared him and by taking that job he had changed his life.

He wrote to me frequently after he left Sioux City; I still have all of the letters. They tell a story.

He was glad to have found a better climate:

> Hate to tell you that the flowers have been up here for a month [early April] and last week the temp was over 70. I do not tell you this in malice; I mention it so you can be thinking about a possible change in your environment someday. Anyone who stays hitched for blizzards all their life should have their head examined.

He obviously went at his work with gusto; that was his style. The magazine soon became under his editorship a respected trade magazine. He also felt that he was improving as a writer:

> I somehow feel that my prose is improving. I am not guilty of as many lapses of grammar as formerly, and unlike Shakespeare I am not using as many adjectives. I may become a writer just about in time to cash in my chips.

But he couldn't have forseen the difficulties that lay ahead of him. Newspapers in the late 50s and early 60s were rapidly changing, partly because of automation and the addition of feature and advertising sections. These changes meant that presses were being engineered so that more and different kinds of work could be done on them. All this of course affected union workers; they were being forced to change too. Always a strong and articulate union man and yet reticent—one who would rather have kept to himself than fight openly for a cause—my father had walked up out of the pressroom and into the bright arena. He would spend less and less of his energy on improving the magazine with feature and historical articles and more and more of his energy on arguing for unionism:

> I am afraid my life is too closely tied with labor propaganda now to ever get much creative writing done.

And again:

> I seem to be a roaring success as a writer-editor of labor publications, but I don't know: If I could find an opportunity open in bootlegging, with a chance to accumulate a sizable chunk of the green stuff the American people worship for god, I would take it. The struggle becomes difficult at times.

I sent him essays I had written for classes and asked him for critiques. He wrote back meticulous sentence-for-sentence comments and offered advice;

> Study hard on punctuation, particularly those goddamn commas. Watch out for unnecessary words, words that add nothing to the sentence but only serve to make it longer. Don't write subjectively. Readers don't really want subdued writing. Critics only tell them they do. Develop your own style.

He was painfully aware of his lack of a formal education:

With my nickel education, I could not compete in a technical race with university graduates, although I probably am better educated in the humanities than most university graduates, and probably a lot of college professors. But there is no market for the person of wide and disparate knowledge.

He compared himself to my professors:

I have no education and five suits; [a college professor] has a good education and one suit.

Sometimes his letters struck a melancholy note:

As for myself, I shall never amount to anything in belles lettres because I missed the fundamentals I would have got had I gone to college. Unless you are a Shakespeare, you must be grounded in the classics. Well, I guess it really doesn't matter now. I would like to see you do something along this line, as I have always wanted one boy in the family to love that sort of thing just for itself if for nothing else. One who loves the classic writers will never be without something to occupy his mind in this worst of all possible worlds.

He was always interested in what I was reading:

As to the old argument on Shakespeare, I, too, am convinced that he wrote the plays. . . If you look hard enough, you could establish the case for Jack Dempsey having written the little poem: 'Ozymandias.'

When I told him I wanted to be an English teacher he wrote;

I envy you, and wish I had a masters and could teach in college.

And again:

> Thomas Wolfe said a professor of English Literature at the U. of North Carolina knew more about Chaucer than the Oxford professors. He used to open his class by saying: 'Can I write a better thesis on Shakespeare than the Oxford professors — yes. Do I have more brains than Shakespeare — yes. Could I have written *King Lear*? No.' Wolfe said he was a truly great teacher.

I had moved back to Sioux City and enrolled in Morningside College, and took a job as night flyboy at the *Journal*. One of my favorite letters starts this way:

> So you took a job as flyboy nights at the *Journal*. Well, it is better than nothing, Dave. Here are a few tips, and don't tell the guys at the *Journal* I sent these tips to you: Don't overload the metal-truck, or it is liable to fall over and wreck the elevator. Be sure the metal truck is centered in the elevator so the handle is not sticking over the edge and can get knocked off. Be careful with the plate dummy, and be careful working around the press. Machinery doesn't give any, and if you get caught, you have had it. And be careful of that back-end feed with the big rolls, Dave. Let the pressmen do their own work back there, and you do your work. Just be careful, period, as it is easy to get crippled for life around a press.

He sent me books to supplement my reading classes:

> I am sending you a new white shirt I got for Christmas but which is too short in the sleeves for me. I hope it fits you. Also in the bundle is a new paperback volume of Voltaire's stuff.

For a birthday, I sent him a book of Thomas Wolfe's letters:
He wrote:

> I sure enjoyed the letters of Tom Wolfe to his
> Mother. He was our American Shakespeare, and
> I predict that someday Americans will be treking
> to Ashville, N.C. to worship at his shrine just as
> the English travel to Stratford to see the Bard's
> home and that of Ann Hathaway.

I had been writing poetry a year or so when I enrolled in a
class in creative writing. I had shown my sister some of my
poems. He wrote:

> Bonnie says you are writing poetry. Is that in
> connection with a class you're taking? I used to
> write poetry too, but not such good stuff.

One of his last letters ended this way:

> I hope you guys are doing all right, Dave.
> Hang on to your pennies, don't monkey around
> with charge accounts, and don't have too many
> kids—that is my advice to the entire world, and
> it is a sure recipe to as much happiness as poss-
> ible in this stinking world.
>
> Much love. Dad

I have no letters dated beyond the fall of 1962. My parents
visited me, my wife, and two kids in Iowa City when I was
studying for my master's degree. That was late in the fall.
When they drove away from our quonset hut in the married
student housing area, that was the last time I saw my father
alive. The following April, on my son's birthday and two days
before the disaster of the submarine *Thresher,* in which more
than a hundred men died, I got a call from my sister in Sioux
City:

"Dave, I got bad news."

"What?" I said, my voice tightening.

"Dad dropped dead this morning in Nashville."

I couldn't speak back into the phone and hung it up to cancel the news. . . .

My wife, sister, uncle, and I drove to Tennessee for the funeral. I stared at my father's hands, placed wing-like on his stomach. They looked too small and white for that large body in a dark blue, double-breasted suit. These weren't the hands I knew—the huge, ink-stained hands I knew. They were the hands of a stranger: delicate, white, small. Too small to be my father's hands.

The long drive back to Iowa City was as gloomy as the drive down to Tennessee. It rained much of the trip. I spent hours with my head buried under a blanket in the back seat. Once when I sat up and looked out the rain-streaked window, I saw my father's face boiling up in a tall thunderhead. It grew and grew. I knew I would remember it a long time. Somewhere near Chicago, in whining traffic, with my face buried so deep it felt like I was speaking inside the car's trunk, I gritted my teeth and promised myself that someday, whatever else happened, I would be a poet, someday *Goddammit* I would be a poet.

The day after we got home I went back to work at the University Hospital. Instead of going directly to the Pharmacy where I worked part-time filling pill bottles and delivering them, I took an elevator eight floors up to the Operating floor. I got out and rushed down the hall, stopping the first man I saw in a green, pressed/wrinkled frock. I had a question for him:

"How is it possible for a man who's never been sick a day in his life to suddenly drop dead of a heart attack?"

He looked at me calmly, spoke calmly:

"There's a thin line between life and death."

We looked at each other a moment. I thanked him, embarrassed by my agitation, my intrusion. I turned and went back to the elevator and dropped through nine clean floors to the Pharmacy.

84

Getting On

"One could not stand and watch very long
without becoming philosophical, without
beginning to deal in symbols and similes,
and to hear the hog-squeal of the universe."
—Upton Sinclair

HIRING GATE

By the end of my sophomore year in college I'd lost my football scholarship, so I needed a job the following summer to support my wife and baby girl. (My wife was working at the time. In the 50s working class culture we came out of, most young married women didn't even dream of having their own careers. If their husbands were fortunate enough to be in college, they had to help "put them through" by working.)

A couple of my high school buddies had gotten jobs at the Sioux City Armour's meat-packing plant, so I decided to give it a try. I knew this would be different from the usual summer construction jobs I'd had. No more working shirtless in the open air. No more getting rained out for days at a time and drinking beer and playing poker while you waited for the unwelcome sun. Once you were there, under that huge, sprawling roof, you were there. That is, if you could *get on.*

Getting on meant getting out of bed at five a.m. and standing in line at the hiring gate until they needed you. It might take an hour, it might take two weeks, it might never happen. Persistence was everything. The hiring gate was a small brick building next to an actual high gate and fence that enclosed the plant. Inside the building (still there, though the plant was razed in the early 60s) was a kind of waiting room with benches along the walls, some folding chairs, and an inner office where the hiring staff worked. The door between the rooms was kept closed; on those several yawning mornings in a row that I stood or sat in that crowded room, very little hiring was going on. Now and then the door opened, faces lit up like lamps, shoulders snapped to attention, and a man with a clip board appeared and called a name or two, and the ones he called followed him back into the office, shutting the door behind them, causing the lamps to go out and the shoulders to slump again, until the door opened, again.

There were two main types of jobs at Armours. First, there were the steady, permanent jobs, most of which had to do with what was called "the chain," which meant keeping up with the flow of meat through the plant: knife work, (only for experts) grading, pulling lard, and so on. This was very demanding work because you had to always be there, alert and concentrated on your particular responsibility. Second, there were the jobs which weren't directly connected with the speed of the meat on pulleys: washing pickling barrels, loading dock, cooler, clean-up, and so on. (The names of jobs or of places in the plant were graphic and accurate. Jobs: "knocking" meant stunning cattle with a "knocking gun" before they were bled; "sticking" meant severing the jugular vein; "shackling" meant hanging the animal upsidedown with winch and chain; "lugging" meant carrying beef on your shoulder; "pulling hides" meant stripping beef hides. Places: "Kill-Floor," "Hog-Kill," "Beef-Kill," "Sheep-Kill," "Beef Trim," "Hide Cellar," "Oleo," "Tank Room," "Offal"—no pun was intended—"Rolling Table," "Sausage," "Ham House," "Freezer," Ice House.")

You had to have signed up beforehand, so that your name was on a list, first come, first served. It would be called only after the names above it had been called and then checked off, either because those before you had been hired or hadn't shown up that morning (in which case, the name was dropped). And yet if you *looked* eager and lively, and were willing to take any job, you might get lucky. This happened because there were certain jobs that most people turned down: Hide

Cellar, Freezer, Tank Room (too messy or smelly or hot or cold; too temporary or permanent). Yet if you turned down too many offers you were considered non-serious, and then you had a tough time getting anything.

The hiring-gate boss, a short, stocky, unperturbed man named Conners, would sometimes open the door, step into the waiting room and say:

"Anybody wanna work in the Hide Cellar? — I need two men." He knew he wouldn't have many, if any, takers for this one.

Two scruffy men might volunteer and follow Conners into the office, or maybe nobody would volunteer, and he would have to fill the jobs with somebody already inside the plant.

Or Connors would step out and say, looking at his clip board: "Coolidge — Beef Cut?"

The man might say, "Here," and follow Connors into the office, or he might say, with reluctance and tension in his voice:

"Nope."

And then other names were called until the job was filled.

The room was full of people like me—tentative, impatient, their faces looking more eager than they themselves actually were, behind the skin. Not wanting to work that bad, but needing the money, I was like a first-time bull rider: part of me wanted to dig in, part of me wanted to just go for a quick ride and no spinning. But after going three or four days without getting even a few hours' work, I decided my best strategy was to take the first thing offered me—anything. Once I was in, if I didn't like it I could always quit; and, better yet, they may give me a good job eventually, from the inside.

Connors, I knew, was smart and could test your seriousness. At first he'd hire you on a day-to-day basis and give you a fairly tough job, say on the kill-floor, where nearly all jobs were chain jobs. If you did well and were liked by the foreman, you might get a time card like the other regulars, and spell out those who called in sick in the morning or who were on vacation. In this way you might stay on for a whole summer. And you wouldn't have to keep going back to Connors for more work.

In the afternoons after the hiring gate had closed for the day, I'd hang around with a few other guys out of work, drinking beer, playing poker, eating tomato sandwiches on white bread smeared with mayonnaise. Or we'd go to the park and play a pick-up game of baseball or softball. And talk about getting on, maybe tomorrow.

On my fourth or fifth morning at the hiring gate I was sitting close to the office door when it suddenly opened for the first time that day, and out walked Connors.

Before he could say anything I stood up.

"Anybody wanna work on the Hog-Kill?—one man," he said.

"Me," I said, and followed him in.

KILL-FLOOR

Walt Whitman and Franz Kafka would have loved the kill-floor, but not to work there. Armour's was known as a "gravity plant": the animals were driven in wooden, slatted chutes that cork-screwed around the building up to the highest floor, the Kill (for short). Here they were stunned (cattle), gassed or shocked (hogs), shackled on pulleys, stuck and bled, split by saws, cut up, and all their parts fell, by simple gravity, through stainless steel holes down to other floors where various other cuts as well as hams, loins, quarters, hides and organs were processed, stored, frozen, pickled, cooled, smoked, or immediately shipped out from the first floor loading dock on trucks and boxcars. This was no modern push button plant where things can go up, down, sideways, across, where loading docks are run by one man with a computer. Everything here started at the top, and then fell. The Floyd River alongside the plant ran blood red all the way to the Missouri.

The noise was relentless, ear-splitting. Horns beeped and blared, whistles shrieked, buzzers buzzed, hooves thudded and banged on steel, chains clinked, cattle bawled or hogs squealed and shrieked, humans yelled, whistled, barrels and tank carts rumbled, shuddered, and banged into tables, knocking guns sputted, pulleys squeaked, saws buzzed and rattled through ribs and vertebrae, hydraulic doors clanged and hissed, bones clanked into pails, knives thunked on chopping blocks, sizzled on stone wheels. . .

How a place could be so organized and yet seem so chaotic, how people could work, joke and laugh together inside such violence — all this as they kept up, almost nonchalantly, with the endless carcasses swinging on rails — is still a wonder to me. In this world, gestures and facial expressions superceded words, and words were usually shouts: obscenities, commands. To speak at length to someone you had to stick your mouth an inch from his ear and shout, and even then he wouldn't get every word, only the monosyllabic gist.

After a day or two I realized the Kill was not for me, except as a watcher. Watching, in fact, was part of my first job — pushing a push-broom, making sure the concrete gutters under the carcasses were free of entrails and blood that would clog them — because I was told to stay out of the way of the knives and to watch certain workers' routines, since I would be broken in on a number of jobs.

I learned very quickly to respect the knives and the men and women using them. They had the highest status of anyone, including the foremen, were given plenty of leeway, and made excellent money. The kill-floor belonged to them. It took years to be able to handle a knife with the consumate skill these displayed. It also took natural hand-eye coordination, a cool temperament, and above all, a sharp knife. The knives were continually steeled, between carcasses, on a long, tapered steel that hung from the worker's belt, along with a wide sheath of extra knives.

Knife work looked tedious and tiring to me. A man or woman stood there, near the bloody gutter, in rubber boots (brown for women, black for men), white rubber apron streaming with blood, white plastic helmet, making the same concise cut with the same concise motions — the knife now flashing, now glittering like the Missouri, now disappearing into white flesh — hour after hour, day after day, year after year, decade after decade. I knew some men who had had the same job — cutting out pituitaries or hearts, trimming beef — for over 30 years. Sharp knives; dull lives. And yet whenever I asked them about their work, they usually said that the day went fast for them, that they were suited to knife work and only knife work. Curiously, they seemed to be the most relaxed and contented people in the packinghouse.

Why were they contented? For at least two reasons. In the 50s, before computers and automation (which would later revolutionize packinghouses) labor unions were strong. When a working person acquired a skill through an apprenticeship and hard work, and had his union card, he had accomplished the ultimate. The highly skilled Armour's workers not only made good hourly wages but also made extra money doing "piece work," that is, turning out more pieces than was required of the average worker. I remember there being a high correlation between the rarity of the skill and the amount of piece work a person got credit for. Of course, the more work turned out, the more money the company made, and so the knife workers and other skilled people were pampered by the bosses.

But there was a more important reason for the knife workers' contentment. Competence breeds integrity. When you are truly good at something—a sport, an art, a job, an avocation—that one thing becomes a part of you, it defines you. The best of the knife men and women reminded me of professional athletes and artists. Their equipment was an extension of their bodies; it had to be constantly checked, handled, and when used, used with exactness and respect. A knife to them was like skiis to the skier, glove and bat to the baseball player, cello to the cellist. They *took* themselves as pros. When they sheathed their knives after a long day, it was an altogether different act from plunking a kitchen knife in a silverware drawer.

My broom job didn't last long. A foreman took me up to the rolling table, which had a bad reputation. (Foremen didn't tell you these things; you learned from your fellow workers. In a union plant in the 50s there were two classes of people: us and them—workers and bosses.)

After the hogs were gassed, stuck and bled, they dropped into an elongated vat of bubbling, boiling water that loosened their bristly hair. A man with a long steel pole moved back and forth above the vat, pushing the bodies, which bobbed like giant hairy apples, along and into a tunnel where they were flung around on a wheel with hundreds of prongs that scraped off the hair. Then they came out onto the waist-high rolling table where I, the "positioner," was standing to catch them and position them for the shackler, about 10 feet away from me, who would shackle each left hind leg to a chain on which, upside down with a slight porcine grin, they began their swinging journey through the kill-floor.

The rolling table was dangerous. You never knew how the hogs—wet, oversized sacks of grain, hot as ovens—would come busting out of the plastic flap of the de-hairing machine. Headfirst, hooffirst, assfirst—you were always guessing. And worse, they were often still whirling. Any moment, you might reach over and grab one leg as it thumped on the steel table, and another would come down on your wrist, snapping it like a twig. But after several hours I discovered a method that was reasonably safe. I would let the hog flop out all the way until its legs were done whirling, and *then* position it. Most men tried to take the legs too soon. Yet my method, too, had its risks. If I let the hog flop and slide out too far without grabbing it, it might slide sideways off the table. Occasionally having a 600-pound sow land in my lap was no picnic, but it was better than broken bones.

Because I had quick, strong hands and enjoyed the athleticism and rhythm of the work, I was good at positioning. It wasn't a job as much as a good workout. I began to take pride in the ease with which I could roll and maneuver the limp, heavy bodies, and a few old timers were amazed that I could be so cool so close to such clamor, such violence of whirling hooves. I was probably too dumb to be scared.

Another job most people dreaded was the snoot machine. I soon learned why. When you stood facing this machine — a small turning wheel — the hog heads came to your left hand one by one, skewered on steel prongs. You had to take each head and set it on the little platform close to the wheel, snoutdown, and two sharp steel teeth came around, stuck into the nostrils and peeled off the "snoot" (like peeling a banana) which dropped into a barrel under the table. Then you took the bloody, skeletal face (a hog's face is nearly all snout) and tossed it into a barrel on your right.

To do this job well, a man needed one more eye and one more hand. The difficult thing was that you had to always be looking to your left so you could see the heads you were grabbing off the prongs, while simultaneously keeping your right hand on the head in front of you, pressing it into the wheel so that the teeth could catch the nostrils. As with picking field corn by hand, you had to be constantly looking at the next object, and the next, never the one already in your hand.

My father, who had worked in a newspaper pressroom for 30 years, had been right with his admonition: *machines don't give.* Several times the teeth ripped off my cotton glove and flapped it to pieces. It would have eaten my bare hand too, if I hadn't been careful. And the machine wouldn't stop. That was the one reality of the kill-floor I couldn't get used to. Once the chain was in motion there was no stopping it. You might as well try to stop a freight train or a blue whale. If you weren't in rhythm with the chain, that was your problem, not the chain's.

The snoot machine psyched me out. Not only did it eat up my gloves, it disabled my right hand. Some of the sow heads were so big and heavy that I had to use both hands to lift them, and then both hands to hold them on the platform. This took too much time and energy and paralyzed my thumb (at first I thought I'd been stricken, that the numbness would spread up my arm to my heart). I had to rest my hand; I got behind. The heads kept piling up, the foreman kept frowning at me, and finally I got so far behind that I could never catch up. Though I didn't show it, I was thrilled when somebody replaced me and I got to go back to the rolling table.

My kill-floor work came to an end after a couple of weeks. I had done well except on the snoot machine, so when I showed up at the hiring gate again I knew it wouldn't be too hard getting on. The question was, what next?

HAULING

A job is much easier when you know you won't have to do it for the rest of your life. That summer at Armour's I enjoyed a feeling of detachment; I was there only for college money and didn't have to bear down. I could do my work, whatever they gave me, and yet be just as much a looker-on as a worker.

It was not that way for others.

One of the clearest, cleanest and most wholesome images I have of the 50s is James Dean in the movie *Rebel Without a Cause,* slowly rolling a cold milk bottle over his forehead. Another is Jim O'Brien, a friend from high school, washing barrels in the fourth-floor Pickling Department. One day I was hauling offal to the tank room—my next job after the kill-floor—and passed through Jim's department. There he was, at 6'3'', a superb basketball player, with a steam hose blasting brine out of a giant pickle barrel. The brine was in chunks around the drain. He saw me, turned off the water, and started talking, he leaning on his barrel, I on my cart handles.

"Hell, Dave," he said, "I got it made."

Then he pulled his billfold out of his back pocket and flipped it open at me.

"Look at this," he said, holding up his brand-new UPWA union card encased in plastic. He read his I.D. number to me.

"All I gotta do is work 35 more years and take the rocking chair money." He acted exactly like a man who believes he's got it made.

I agreed he had it made.

We talked for several more minutes and I had to go.

About a year later the Pickling Deaprtment shut down; three years after that, Armour's was levelled to the ground and O'Brien, at 24 and with a wife and two kids already, was looking for work. In the 20 odd years since that day I talked with him on the fourth floor, Jim has worked at many jobs, including shoveling popcorn at a popcorn company, driving a milk truck, and janitor work. He did last 10 years as a janitor, but that company went bankrupt in the early 80s.

Recently I saw him in a tavern when I was in town visiting relatives. We were in a booth sipping tap beer and eating potato chips. His face had lost some light, as I'm sure mine had too, and we were both a little paunchy.

"It's tough starting to drive a truck again at 42," he said. I agreed it must be tough.

As we talked, that scene at Armour's all those years ago flashed into my mind: Jim standing there with a hose, the big round pickling barrel steaming and shining, chunks of brine around the drain, and then the youthful exuberance of his words about having it made, and the rocking chair money. I kept wondering if he remembered too.

For the balance of the summer I had mostly hauling jobs. Loading, hauling, and unloading carts were easy tasks compared to chain work. I could go more or less at my own pace, the bosses were less anxious, and I could get around the plant and see friends in other departments, and watch other operations. All of us haulers appreciated the long waits at the slow, open, dangerous, antiquated elevators (you had to pull the cable *down* to make the elevator come *up* to you). You might get lucky and have to wait 30 minutes or more. Then you could rap with others, smoke, get pop, peanuts and beef jerkies at the snack shop, or stick your head in the freezer to cool off. Because Armour's was such a huge plant with such a variety of hauling going on between departments so distant from each other, your boss couldn't chew you out for taking 45 minutes to deliver something.

All this, of course, tended to be inefficient and wasteful, and gravity plants were fast becoming obsolete in the late 50s. They would soon be replaced by smaller, mechanized plants in rural areas or small towns where labor was cheaper and unions weaker or non-existent. I remember sensing frustration and impatience on the company's side. Superintendents were pressuring foremen, foremen were taking it out on workers: *speed up the chain, put out more work.*

So-called efficiency experts in white frocks, with clipboards and stop watches were dispatched around the plant to determine whether jobs could be done more efficiently. The union workers resented them, considered them eggheads, dreamers. The workers knew there were always exigencies — kinks in the chain, government inspectors looking over your shoulder, ready to red-tag anything that wasn't clean.

(With a perspective of some 20 years, I now realize that the gap between workers and company was unnecessarily wide. The union was often pushy and arrogant, and the company, knowing the plant was outmoded and that it *could* make more money, was often greedy.)

The efficiency experts didn't bother us haulers, only those rooted to the floor in their routines. My jobs took me all over the plant, and much of what I saw — places, people, and their jobs — has stayed with me.

The man in the tank room, for instance, who took my carts of offal. He worked his eight-hour day inside hissing steam, Armour's version of Hell. The steam was his white floor and his white ceiling. It kept belching up out of the two rows of tank holes after he jerked open their iron lids. I rarely saw him. (Did the steam make him shy, an animal in fog?) I just got glimpses of him.

But I can still put him together. He was shirtless with a bulging hairy chest, a filthy seed hat. His back and shoulders were the color of, must have *felt* like, boiled lobster. His biceps, constantly working, were round and seamed like hardballs. When I got close to him I noticed he was always grinning. (Was there some secret, speechless joy he couldn't help?) He never spoke. He worked by himself, without breaks. I never saw him puffing on a cigarette, leaning against the handles of a tankage cart, complaining about the pay or the heat.

The heat was too much for me. I could stay in that stinking Hell no longer than it took to dump my load of condemned heads or kidneys or bellies. I took a deep breath before I went in. I rolled my cart in fast and looked around for him, caught his finger pointing to the least full tank. By the time I got there the lid was open and his pitchfork hands were ready. I tipped my cart over the hole as the steam belched up under us, swirling and relentless, hammering my face and forehead. He was on his knees. He stuck his hands deep inside the cart, up past his elbows, up to his red shoulders and beyond, scooping, pulling, forking, jerking everything out. His back and arms and neck were matted with guts and worms. I knew he was grinning. His head kept nodding with his extreme motions, as if he figured he could grab joy out of anything I brought him.

There were pleasanter rooms to enter. Whenever it rained and I was in the vicinity, I would duck into the condemned Ice House, a small, unlighted room just off the Beef-Kill. It was cool and I enjoyed sitting on the wooden bench and listening to the rain hitting the tin roof just over my head. I had also heard hot rumors about couples sneaking in there for sex, and so always expected to surprise somebody when I banged the heavy steel latch with the heel of my hand and forced open the thick, insulated door, letting in light. Even today, whenever I hear rain on a roof, I often imagine a man and a woman hugging on a wooden bench in a secret room, the rain's skeleton fingers tapping on a tin roof, in the condemned dark of Armour's.

The luggers on the loading dock were marvelous to watch, the ideal embodiment of brute strength joined with grace and timing. Many had been football linemen in high school, and some had taken the job as a conditioner for college football.

They had to be strong enough to hold a leg of beef on their shoulders and carry it 30 or 40 feet into a boxcar, some days going as long as 12 hours. I had never before, and haven't since, seen so many dominant males in one gang. Unconscious, aloof, sociable among themselves, boisterous, bawdy and zany, they loved to clown around and display. They constantly challenged each other with mock stares and shouts and fisticuffs.

Six or seven made a crew. Each one took his turn walking under a platform, with a man standing on it, that was wheeled to each open boxcar on the dock. Placing his padded shoulder under a slab of beef hanging from the main carcass above the platform, he walked forward a few steps with the beef as it swung out, then walked backward a few steps as it swung back, then forward again and this time, just as the meat reached the peak of its swing, the man on the platform freed it with a quick slice of his knife, and the lugger was under the leg and moving with it, balancing it the way a Swahili woman balances a heavy jug of water on her head.

The rhythm of lugging was difficult to master, but no lugger would last long without mastering it. A man couldn't simply lift the meat all day on strength alone; he had to go with the swing, marry his weight to the bulk and weight of the meat. Lugging was a dance of the burly.

On breaks, if I couldn't find a friend around I would often sit on the fire escape outside the Beef-Kill and watch the cattle getting knocked. There was always talk that this grim work (like sticking) drove a person crazy if he didn't take periodic breaks of several weeks. And more talk about those big steers and bulls that hadn't been stunned enough — because their skulls were thick as bank vaults — coming to on the floor and charging anything they saw, and everybody quailing away in all directions. And also that berserk bull back in the 30s (when knocking was done with sledge hammers, hence the word) that charged right through an open window and plunged through eight floors of air onto the sidewalk. (Some insisted he got up and kept charging; some that it wasn't the fall that killed him, but the sudden stop.)

The knockers seemed healthy to me, and knocking a clean, safe job, if loud. The prodders had to be good. They moved

97

back and forth on the catwalk above the loading chute just outside the plant, jolting the cattle with electric prodding sticks, toward the pair of knocking pens. The prodders had to be nimble enough to separate the animals so that only one at a time got into a pen.

The knocker then, on his catwalk above the cattle, punched a red button and the gate slammed shut. The penned animal lurched, bucked, and then when it discovered it couldn't walk any further, hesitated. The man reached down with his .22 pistol that shot out an inch-and-a-half-long spike (the gun looked more like a linoleum stapler) put it about a half inch from the white forehead that appeared to have been fashioned on the moon with ballpean hammers, and pulled the trigger. The animal dropped, breathless, its legs in motion, banging the pen's sides as if trying to run through a steel wall. Then the man punched a green button and the floor collapsed and the animal slid out onto the slick kill-floor for the shackler with his chain and pulleys.

The animal was far from dead. You can't kill a 1,500-pound steer with a jolt to the brain — it took awhile for death to do its job. All its programmed life the steer had been following a long trail and looking straight ahead, and then suddenly its legs were knocked out from under it, and then it was upside-down, hoof-over-head and swinging with its tongue hanging out, and then its jugular vein was severed.

Years later, I wrote a poem about the "bred-for slaughter" as James Dickey called them, the endless cattle that go on dying in one's memory even after the packing plant is gone:

> dying is a shy habit here
> that goes on always:
> the one with the face of a friend
> the one with the mushroomed eye
> the one with the limp
>
> I am near them all
> though the kill-floor heavens fall

NIGHT CLEAN-UP

Summer too was stunned and dying, the regulars were coming back from vacations, and the hiring had slowed down. I lost my hauling job but got on at night, three to eleven p.m., in the Oleo Department.

My job was to make things new and shiny again, my tool a steam hose (or, blow hose). The water was so hot it was constantly changing to steam, blowing insanely, and scalding my hand, so I had to adjust the temperature for a hot spray that could cut caked lard on floors and machines. This was a snap job, the easiest I've ever had, the most solitary, and in certain ways the most satisfying. Night pay was 10 or 12 cents-per-hour better than day pay, and I was furnished gloves and boots by the company.

I liked the work also because I could turn, by myself, a messy department into a sparkling one in a matter of a few hours. (Nothing shines like stainless steel under light bulbs!) I've never had another job in which I could see the results of my efforts so readily, from start to finish. And all I needed was a steam hose and hot water.

At night, in the dimly-lit places, the cockroaches living inside the walls came out—feeler-first, probing, then whole, reddish-brown, long as fingers, hard as sea shells. I blew them away and scalded them, but they kept coming back, one by one, waving their antennae, zipping down the wall, across the hot floor, under another wall. They tumbled, skidded, and flew in the spray, but they kept coming back. How *unlike* the cattle they were in their tenacity and resiliency and individuality, and how *like* the cattle they were too: kill one and a million more were ready to take its place—to feel, zip, disappear under walls.

With hours to spare after I cleaned up the Oleo, I walked around the plant and talked with other clean-up men, raided the ham house and sausage department, drank pop and ate peanuts. Mostly I read in the foreman's office, my feet propped up on the desk. I read Thomas Wolfe's "The Lost Boy," and cried. I read some Hemingway stories, and Faulkner's "Spotted Horses." When I got to the scene in which the crazy, scared circus horse "scrabbled up" the wagon tongue into the laps of two sleeping women, I laughed so hard I literally fell off the chair.

The only drawback to night work was the hours. I had been on a softball team that summer; now the play-off games that would decide the league winners were going on (at night) and here I was working the clean-up shift at Armour's.

I became a little arrogant, figuring I could do anything I wanted to as long as I got my work done. For instance, why not sneak out, as others did: crawl under the gate behind the plant, walk the railroad tracks, play a game, and get back under the gate before punching out for the night?

My scheme worked for four or five nights, but on the last one when I got back, the night plant superintendent was waiting for me in the office.

"Are you Evans?" he asked. He was very serious, in a starched white frock.

"Yes."

"I've been looking for you all night — where you been?"

He had me. I tried to weasel out of it, but every place I mentioned I was, he had checked out and recorded in his log book.

He wrote something else down in his book, and left.

The next day when I came through the gate a little before 3:00 to punch in, the superintendent was waiting again. This time he was calmer, but firm.

"Pick up your check, Evans," was all he had to say.

EPILOGUE

Having lived for a time in one world and then left it for another, all of us search for bridges, links that keep the old worlds alive, if only in memory. The shattered pumpkin, for instance, that had been hurled out of Sleepy Hollow by the Headless Horseman into a bright morning of the other world of Ichabod Crane, the school teacher.

One night I thought I had found my pumpkin.

About a year ago in Sioux City, back to visit, I was drinking beer with some old buddies in a honky-tonk joint on the West Side. I was watching a man playing pool, wondering if he was the man in the tank room at Armour's. The same grin, the same filthy seed hat, and jerky movements. Or was it the beer that made him look like he had just walked right out of Hell?

I approached him with my beer, the only way to approach a stranger playing pool in a beer joint in Sioux City, Iowa.

"Did you ever work at Armour's," I said, having to shout above the noise.

"No," he said, shouting back in the pinched voice of a man who rarely speaks. "But I got a cousin used to work in the packinghouse in Spencer." Then I saw he was too young. That was 20 years ago.

He chalked his cue, levelled his aim over the table, shot a ball in a corner pocket. He straightened up, stepped close to me again, standing his cue on end.

"I been mistaken for a lot of guys," he shouted, grinning more. "Just last week this guy walked up to me and says: 'Ain't you the guy that screwed my wife?'

'Hell,' I said, 'I don't even *know* her.' "

About the Author

David Evans was born and raised in Sioux City, Iowa. He has a bachelor's degree from Morningside College, a master's degree from the University of Iowa, and another master's — in creative writing — from the University of Arkansas. He was a Bread Loaf Scholar in 1975. He received a National Endowment for the Arts writing grant in 1976, and a writing grant from the South Dakota Arts Council in 1980. He is the author of three books of poems: *Among Athletes* (Folder Editions, 1971); *Train Windows* (Ohio University Press, 1976); *Real and False Alarms* (Bk MK Press, University of Missouri-Kansas City, 1984); He is General Editor and Writer for *What the Tallgrass Says* (Center for Western Studies, 1981). He is the editor of *New Voices in American Poetry* (Winthrop Publishers, 1973), and co-editor of *The Sport of Poetry/The Poetry of Sport* (SDSU Foundation, 1978). He is an experienced racquetball player, and has recently taken up Shotokan Karate. He and his wife Jan live in Brookings, South Dakota. They have three children.